LUCKY *GO* HAPPY

LUCKY *GO* HAPPY

MAKE HAPPINESS HAPPEN!

Paul van der Merwe

For Corlia, Morné, and Ruhan,

For the happy moments you give me.

Money makes the world go round;
however, happiness greases the axle.
Without this lubricant, life will seize.

Contents

Preface

Being happy is not important. It is *extremely* important. In fact, being happy is so important to us that we pursue it through every single thing we do, through everything we have ever done, and through everything we will ever do.

Sometimes we pursue happiness directly. We watch a movie or go on holiday because doing these things makes us happy. We expect happiness as the outcome.

Most of the time, however, we pursue happiness subconsciously. We do things not to be happy but rather to *avoid* unhappiness. By avoiding unhappiness, we are left feeling happy or content. At least that is how we reason subconsciously.

Take eating and working for example. We are not happy when we are hungry. We then eat to still the hunger, but subconsciously we are eating to make the associated unhappiness go away. We are actually eating to move from our unhappy state to a happy one. We eat to be happy.

Similarly, we are unhappy when we do not have money. We then work to earn money so we can eradicate the associated unhappiness. By eradicating the unhappiness, we are moving toward happiness. We are therefore working so we can be happy.

People not working for the money are also pursuing happiness. However, they do it more directly. The love for what they do, or the feeling of giving without compensation, gives them a kick, and that is what makes them happy.

Since everything we do is in pursuit of happiness, one would expect society to focus a lot more on understanding this emotion. After all, that is ultimately the reason for everything we do.

Rather than teaching us how happiness works, society presents us with stepping-stones on the road to happiness, such as: if you study this, you will get that job, and *then* you will be happy. If you own this, you will impress your friends, and *then* you will be happy. If you eat healthy and exercise regularly, you will lose those pounds, and *then* you will be happy.

These stepping-stones do give us a shot at some happiness, but they do not help us understand happiness. We need to understand happiness, and not the stepping-stones, if we want to make happiness happen.

Happiness is a complex puzzle. Every chapter of *Lucky Go Happy* covers a piece of that puzzle and provides insights into the workings of happiness. The chapters should therefore not be read as if they build up to a big reveal in the final chapter.

Happiness does not work that way. It is all about the journey and not the destination.

Acknowledgment

The storylines in chapters 13 and 17 are loosely based on stories that my father told me as a child. The true origins and authors of the original stories are unknown, and the author wishes to acknowledge the authors of the original works.

1

A Beautiful but Boring Life

Lucky is no ordinary rat. He is happily married to his only wife. They have two children, ages two and five. During the week, Lucky works from nine to five, while his wife looks after the children.

Lucky showed enormous potential as a young rat. Everyone expected him to climb the corporate ladder like other rats, by starting as a runner in a laboratory. From an early age, however, he excelled at math, and it soon became evident that his passion for numbers would see him follow a different career.

Lucky worked hard in school and graduated at the top of his class. He received the prestigious World Wildlife Fund study grant to further his education.

Upon completion of his degree in applied mathematics, he started teaching students from all walks, crawls, and flights of life at the African Bushveld Technical Academy.

Lucky finds immense satisfaction in what he does. He has devoted many extra hours to his students and to the academy.

Lucky was promoted to senior lecturer two rainy seasons ago. The new role has been fulfilling and helped to repay most of the mortgage on their upmarket den not far from work.

Apart from his passion for numbers, Lucky is also a part-time writer. He gained acclaim across the Bushveld region with the publication of his first book, *Surviving Global Warming: Raft-Building Techniques for Wingless Mammals.*

Lucky has a very good life, albeit monotonous at times. Arriving home from work, he helps with the afternoon routine of feeding and bathing the children. After the customary bedtime stories, Lucky spends a few hours with his wife to reflect on the day and to discuss their hopes and dreams for the future.

Weekends mostly involve extended family commitments or attending children's birthday parties. Birthdays are a big thing in the rat fraternity and occupy most of their weekends. On off weekends, they break away for a family camping trip or throw a few crickets on the barbecue with some friends.

Once a year, leave permitting, Lucky and his family spend their summer breakaway at their holiday den on the banks of the Mamba River. Here the focus falls on spending quality time with the kids. Fishing and swimming are the highlights during the day, while bonfires and stargazing fill their nights. During these weekends, the lecturer makes way for the dad.

It is a good life indeed. It is a life to be grateful for, but not one to be ecstatic about. This worries Lucky. There is so much to be thankful for, yet something is missing. He knows he is no ordinary rat, yet somehow he is leading an ordinary life. Is there something more to come, or is this it? Is this how he will spend the remainder of his life?

Lucky has pondered these questions so many times before. This time is different though. This time he is on the eve of an adventure that will change his life and the way he looks at it forever.

2

Lucky Is Summoned

It is a hot and humid Monday afternoon in the Bushveld. Conditions are perfect for a wildcat thunderstorm even though the rainy season had ended. Fifteen minutes before the end of class, Lucky is immersing himself in the theorem of Pythagoras.

Totally unannounced, and with the speed and ferocity of a lightning bolt, the classroom door swings open and crashes into the wall.

Lucky fractures the chalk and swings around from the blackboard. Several pupils fall from their chairs as they are torn from their daydreams in which Pythagoras played no part.

Pigeon stands in the doorway. His feathers are ruffled and his eyes even bigger than the twenty-six pairs staring back at him.

"Lion … wants to see you … now!" Pigeon utters between gasps for air.

"Class dismissed!" shouts Lucky as he storms out of the room. Lion is one of his former pupils. Moreover, he has been Lion's confidant since the Trophy Hunters took Lion's father in the year of the Big Drought.

In spite of their close-knit relationship, Lion still is the king of the Bushveld. He is a fair but demanding leader. No one dares dawdle once summoned to appear before the king.

"Hundred hungry hyenas!" Lucky cries as he pulls into the afternoon rush-hour stampede. "Traffic is definitely becoming worse. There are just too many animals reaching old age since those human conservationists moved into this area," he mumbles while overtaking a tortoise plodding along in the fast lane.

About an hour after abandoning his class, Lucky arrives at Lion's den. He immediately walks up to Lion who is peacefully perched on an old termite mound. Lion stares across the savannah with his big amber eyes; his silhouette etched against a red African sunset.

Lucky clears his throat to announce his arrival. He looks up at Lion to gauge the purpose of his summons, but Lion continues staring into the distant beyond without uttering a word.

Not wanting to interrupt the moment, Lucky joins in with a stare of his own. His heart drops down from his throat as he switches from rush-hour stampede to total serenity.

And so, the two of them sit side by side and in total silence until the red-orange sky makes way for a million bright flickering stars that gaze down upon them.

3

Lion's Predicament

"How long have we known each other, Lucky?" Lion finally breaks the silence. His voice is a lot calmer than usual.

"We met two rainy seasons before the year of the Great Drought, Lion," Lucky says. "So that means we've known each other for twelve rainy seasons."

"Yes, and you have seen me grow into what I am today. You know the Lion behind the wild mane and ferocious roar. You have probably taught me everything I know, other than hunting impala of course."

"Where could this be going?" Lucky thinks. "Lion is a lot more brain than brawn tonight. Maybe this is a good time to suggest my solution for the rush-hour stampede. If only lionesses hunted more often, the roads wouldn't be so full of animals, meaning less traffic congestion."

"Something is terribly wrong with me, Lucky," Lion says, "but I can't put my paw on it. I'm not sick or hungry or anything. I just miss being happy. It's not that I'm *un*happy. It's just that I'm *not* happy.

"I have a good life and so much to be thankful for. In spite of all my blessings, Lucky, I'm still not happy. An empty feeling has become part of me."

"I don't quite follow you, Lion," Lucky replies, somewhat hesitantly. He searches Lion's face for a clue to where the discussion is going.

"Everything we do is done for one of two reasons," Lion responds. "We either do something because it makes us happy, or we do something to *avoid* unhappiness. Either way, the objective of everything we do is to be happy."

"Okay, now you've really lost me," Lucky replies.

"Think about it, Lucky," Lion says. "First, there are the *nice*-to-dos. We do these things because they make us happy. We expect happiness as the result. We play with the kids, watch the sunset, read a hunting magazine, or take a dip in the river because we like doing it. Doing these things give us pleasure and make us happy.

"Secondly, there are the *have*-to-dos," Lion continues. "Take eating for example. We're not happy when we're hungry. We then eat to still the hunger, but subconsciously we're eating to make the associated unhappiness go away. We're actually eating to move from our unhappy state to a happy one. We eat to be happy.

"Similarly, we're unhappy when we're out of shape. We then exercise to get into shape in an attempt to move from being unhappy to being happy. We're therefore exercising in order to be happy."

"Now I see where you're going with this!" Lucky says. "So your argument is that we work to be happy? We're unhappy when we don't have money. We then work to earn money so we can eradicate the associated unhappiness. By eradicating the unhappiness, we're moving toward happiness. We're therefore working so we can be happy?"

"Exactly!" Lions purrs with a sense of accomplishment. "Everything we do ultimately has the same objective. That objective is to be happy, either directly or indirectly, by avoiding unhappiness."

"I'm not sure how I can help with this," Lucky says with a puzzled look on his face.

"My problem, Lucky," says Lion, "is that I have read many books on topics such as eating right, exercising, and excelling at my job. Although these books addressed the subject matter, they completely missed the point. They cover the stepping-stones to happiness but not happiness itself.

"I'm not interested in stepping-stones anymore, Lucky. They are only secondary objectives. I need to understand our primary goal. I need to understand happiness. If I understand how happiness works, then surely I can make happiness happen, right?"

Before Lucky can respond, Lion continues. "I need you to travel throughout my kingdom and ask every animal you meet what happiness is to them. I'm hoping their collective knowledge on happiness will restore my inner peace. You must report back to me before the start of the rainy season."

The discussion ends with the same silence it started with. Lion has spoken his mind. It is a big request, and Lucky contemplates the consequences of declining it. He stares across the savannah as if looking for an answer. I will have to do this, he eventually concludes.

The pressure mounts as the silence drags on. "Why will they share anything with me?" Lucky finally responds. "I'm a tiny rat. Animals might be too busy, or simply not interested in helping me."

"Take this," Lion says, handing Lucky a tuft of hair from his golden mane. "This way they will know it's I who sent you. They will know the consequences of not helping you."

As Lucky heads home, his mind is in turmoil. "What a crisis! This was supposed to be just another Monday. How will my family cope without me? It's too long to be away from home. My students will fall behind. Where will I sleep at night?" he thinks, trying to make sense of the crisis that has befallen him.

When Lucky arrives home, the children are already asleep. His wife is reading a book in bed. Lying down beside her, he shares the conversation he had with Lion. When she learns of Lucky's brief, tears well up in her eyes.

"I couldn't say no to Lion, dear," says Lucky. "He is the king of the Bushveld, and he needs my help. I must honor and obey his request however arduous it may seem."

With these words, they close their eyes and start drifting off. Their minds race ahead to sunrise as they hold each other's claws. Tomorrow at dawn, the rising sun will mark the separation of their lives for a while.

4

The Elephant Crisis

As the sun rises, Lucky emerges from his den with a backpack full of necessities for his trip—a sleeping bag, firefly lantern, mosquito net, snake repellent, and a lunch pack that his wife prepared for him.

With a hug and a "Love you, dear; see you soon," Lucky starts his journey into the vast expanse of the Bushveld.

Two hours into his journey, Lucky spots Elephant beside a water hole. "What an intimidating figure," Lucky thinks. He nervously feels his pockets for the tuft of mane Lion gave him as travel insurance.

Walking up to Elephant, Lucky notices that both of his tusks are missing. Only short stumps remain on either side of his massive head.

Lucky introduces himself, making sure that Lion gets a mention. "Good morning, Elephant. My name is Lucky, and I'm on a fact-finding mission for Lion."

"And a good morning to you," Elephant replies as he continues to chew on a bushel of grass. "What kind of facts are you hoping to find?"

"Happiness," Lucky answers. "I need to find out what makes animals happy. Is there any wisdom you can share with me?"

"That's a tough one," Elephant says while uprooting another bundle of grass with his trunk. "It may not be exactly what you're looking for, but I do have a story I can share with you. I'm sure it will help you with your quest."

"I'm a surgeon," Elephant begins. "I used to practice homeopathic medicine when I still had my tusks, you see."

"What happened?" Lucky asks the inevitable question.

"Love happened. The things we do for love," Elephant shyly sighs. "Both my tusks broke off in a fight with another bull over an elephant cow. It wasn't just any old cow. She was the matriarch-in-waiting. The fight was definitely worth it, even though the price I paid was very high.

"Anyway, I used my tusks to earn a living as a homeopath. They were the tools of my trade. I used them to dig up roots and to peel bark from medicinal trees. After drying them, I placed the roots and bark into a hollowed-out section of bedrock. I used the ends of my tusks to grind them into a fine powder in this bedrock.

"I mixed these fine powders in various combinations to make my medicines. My medicine treated anything from tuberculosis to predator-induced anxiety syndrome, or PIAS, as it's more commonly known.

"After losing my tusks, I could no longer dig for roots or peel bark from trees. I was unable to make the medicine that was the cornerstone of my practice. I started losing patients and eventually had to close my doors. I was officially unemployed. I couldn't pay the bills or do the thing I loved most: helping other animals.

"I was faced with the biggest crisis of my life. The weight on my shoulders grew heavier with each passing day. All of that changed, however, the day I met the weirdest-looking creature I had ever seen.

"He called himself Panda. He had the colors of a zebra, the body-fat percentage of a hippo, and fur like a baboon. Panda visited the African Bushveld as part of a habitat-scouting delegation from China. Our local cuisine gave him severe stomach cramps. When Panda's condition didn't improve, he was referred to me by a former patient.

"I was unable to help Panda as a result of my crisis. I told him my unfortunate story, as I didn't want to appear unwilling to help a stranger.

"Panda then told me that a crisis had the potential for a positive outcome," Elephant continues. "Panda added that the word *crisis* is written in Chinese using two different characters. The characters look something like this."

Elephant shows Lucky the tree where Panda scratched them into the bark:

Tree 4.1 – Crisis Written in Chinese

"The first character represents danger, while the second character represents opportunity," Elephant says. "The word crisis is thus literally written as danger-opportunity.

"Panda explained that there was an element of danger in every crisis, but also an opportunity. Until Panda shared this wisdom with me, I had focused all my energy on the danger element of my crisis. I was thinking about what I had lost and how things had changed for the worse since losing my tusks.

"Panda asked if I ever considered the opportunities that my crisis presented. The thought of opportunities arising from my crisis never even crossed my mind.

"Anyway, I referred Panda to a former colleague of mine for treatment of his stomach cramps. I then purposefully tried to think of opportunities associated with *not* having tusks. Initially my thoughts were empty. Elephants are meant to have tusks, so my thoughts continued to stray down the danger element of the crisis.

"Slowly but surely, however, some opportunities entered my mind.

"First, having no tusks gave me access to the young and succulent leaves that other elephants couldn't reach with their tusks in the way. Secondly, I had the option of becoming a surgeon. Previously, my tusks prevented me from getting close enough to patients to make incisions.

"The third benefit was no longer having chronic neck pain from carrying those heavy tusks around. I was also saving a small fortune on toothpaste, not to mention the time it took to brush my tusks every morning.

"That discussion with Panda changed my life. Today I'm a successful surgeon only because I saw an opportunity in the crisis that came my way," Elephant concludes.

"Not only a successful surgeon, but a brilliant motivational speaker!" Lucky replies. "When Lion gave me this task, it had crisis written all over it. Up until now, I have been focusing on the danger element of my crisis.

"I'm stressing about being away from home. I'm worried about the safety of my family. I also fear that my students will fall behind. However, you have opened my eyes and my thoughts, Elephant.

"Come to think of it, I now see an opportunity of visiting new and exciting places. I can meet interesting animals and learn firsthand about a topic I have often wondered about myself."

"I'm glad I could help!" Elephant obliges while patting Lucky on the head with his trunk.

"I'll remember your advice and convey it to Lion," Lucky says. He picks up his backpack and heads off with renewed purpose into the great unknown.

5

Cycles of the Blue Wildebeest

With Elephant's advice still fresh in his mind, Lucky heads out of a thicket of Mopani trees into an open patch of grassland. Lucky sees Blue Wildebeest, roughly in the middle of the patch, and changes course to meet up with him.

Blue Wildebeest hardly notices Lucky and continues to graze with Lucky standing right beside him. Unaware that these animals eat almost every waking moment, Lucky politely waits for Blue Wildebeest to finish his meal before introducing himself.

Eventually, Lucky interrupts the sound of grass being ground into pulp with a simple "Hi there, my name is Lucky." This seems to have the desired effect, and Blue Wildebeest lifts his head to signal the end of his meal—for the moment at least.

"I am Blue Wildebeest. Care for some grass? There's plenty for both of us," he says.

After a quick "no thanks," Lucky explains the purpose of his visit.

"So is there anything you can share with me?" Lucky finally asks.

"Yes there is, Lucky. You see, I have the most boring job in the world. I supposedly am a landscape architect. Quite a fancy job title, but practically all it entails is mowing the grasslands of the savannah. With all the good rains we've been having, it's a full-time job.

"I need to keep these grasslands in pristine condition for the human tourists who visit all year round. Do you have any idea how it feels to be working, eating grass for twelve hours a day, five days a week?"

"No, not really," Lucky replies. "I have worked long hours before, but eating grass? I will leave you to it then."

"But I thought you wanted to learn about happiness," Blue Wildebeest says with a puzzled look on his face.

"I do, but your life seems too uneventful. With all due respect, you seem to be bordering on depression, so I doubt whether you have anything to contribute," Lucky responds.

"On the contrary, my friend. All that time spent eating grass leaves lots of free time for the mind. I spend this time wisely to ponder many things, including happiness," Blue Wildebeest says.

Lucky stops dead in his tracks.

"For blue wildebeests like me, happiness comes in two cycles," the large, bearded antelope says. "There is a weekly cycle and a yearly cycle. Sadly, we only allow ourselves to be happy during a part of each of these cycles."

"This sounds interesting," Lucky thinks. So he picks a spot on the grass where he has full view of Blue Wildebeest.

"During the week, we work," Blue Wildebeest says. "We eat grass for five days of the week and for twelve hours every day. We're working all the time and can't wait for the weekend to arrive. Weekends are our happy times. Lionesses are so tied up on weekends with shopping, kiddie parties, and sports events for the cubs that they don't bother us one little bit.

"The other great thing about weekends is that we don't have to eat any grass. We can simply chew the cud. Weekends are really, really great—a time to take a break, relax, and be happy.

"In the yearly cycle, we have a two-week summer holiday. During this holiday, we take part in the Great Migration. That's the happiest time of the whole year. We get to travel and meet up with relatives and old friends. A few lucky ones even get to star in a National Geographic documentary. A bit of fame if you catch my drift.

"Do you see the problem with living life this way, Lucky?" Blue Wildebeest says, with his vision of fame making way for reality.

"Yes I do. You will either be eaten by lions or die of malnutrition from eating only grass," Lucky responds.

"No, no, no!" Blue Wildebeest says, disgruntled. "The problem is that we *postpone* our happiness! We've come to believe we can only be happy on weekends or during holidays. We rarely give ourselves a chance to be happy during the workweek, or when we're not on holiday.

"The math is quite simple here, Lucky," Blue Wildebeest says after pausing for a moment. "Every week, we only allow ourselves to be happy for two out of the seven days. That equates to being happy only thirty percent of the week! Every year, we only allow ourselves happiness during the two-week holiday. That's two out of the fifty-two available weeks, or permitting ourselves to be happy only four percent of the year.

"However you look at these low percentages, we're failing. We're failing to be happy simply because we're not granting ourselves more time to be happy.

"Sadly, weekends and holidays also have unhappy moments. This means our *actual* happiness will be even less than the thirty percent weekly, or four percent yearly, time we *allow* ourselves to be happy."

Lucky stares out in front of him as he takes it all in. "That's both shocking and brilliant! But what can we do to fix this?" he asks.

"My herd has developed two methods. The objective is to *allow* ourselves more time to be happy. We focus on the five days of the week and the fifty weeks of the year that we generally wish away in anticipation of happiness to come. We have a saying that the bigger a spider's web, the better his chances are of catching something.

"Back to the two methods," Blue Wildebeest continues. "First, we deliberately look for happiness that was always there, but overlooked as we set our sights on weekends. For example, take watching the sunset over the tree line or watching shooting stars at night. Knowing there is enough to eat and seeing your kids playing silly games in the long grass.

"We made a conscious decision to notice and appreciate these small, everyday things in our lives. This helped us to be content during the week, and strangely we drew happiness from this deep sense of satisfaction.

"Our second method required a change in routine. With a life of constant grazing, sleeping, and grazing some more, we had very little chance of being happy during the week unless we changed our routine."

"On Tuesdays, we now have a Chefs' Evening when we share different recipes for grass. Wednesday night is Horror Night when we take turns sharing some close encounters with predators.

"Thursday nights are the best of them all. We play Mock-the-Croc, which almost rivals the Great Migration in terms of having a good time. While the herd is watching from a safe distance, one of us pretends to be injured and moans and groans while rolling around on the bank of the river.

"The crocs, thinking it will be an easy catch, come waltzing out of the water with that macho, bodybuilder-like wiggle of theirs. Seeing the crocs' jaws drop when the uninjured animal jolts away is truly priceless. We crack ourselves up every time. We can never make out whether their jaws drop in disbelief or because of hunger.

"Our new routine during the workweek has given us something new to enjoy and look forward to. We now have more potential happy time than when we lived for weekends only. This has helped to increase our overall happiness."

"Your advice ties in nicely with what Elephant told me about a crisis," Lucky says. "You made a conscious decision to change your routine. Sometimes, however, a crisis forces that change in routine, which then has the potential to increase our happiness. Thanks for sharing this with me."

"You're most welcome, Lucky," Blue Wildebeest obliges. "Hopefully my story will help you and Lion."

It is with a strong sense of accomplishment that Lucky bids farewell to Blue Wildebeest. As he continues on his quest, he cannot help to see the smile on Lion's face when he shares what he has learned.

6

Hyena Selling Unhappiness

Lucky wakes up to a hyena laughing as if he had just pulled off the best practical joke ever.

"This I need to see," Lucky thinks. "Laughter like that can only come from a very happy animal. I'm sure he can teach me lots about happiness."

Lucky gets out of his makeshift bed and heads in the direction of the laughter. The laughter continues to grow louder until Lucky eventually spots the hyena.

"Nothing hilarious that meets the eye," Lucky wonders. So he walks up to the hyena to introduce himself.

"Hi there. My name is Lucky, and Lion has sent me on a quest to learn more about happiness. Do you have any words of wisdom on the topic?" Lucky says.

Hyena bursts out laughing again. After a while, his gasps for air die down enough for him to mutter, "Funny little guy. Really, really funny."

Eventually, the hysterical laughter dies down a bit, giving Hyena the opportunity to attempt longer sentences.

"I am Hyena. My business is to make people *un*happy, so I find it quite amusing that you want my advice on happiness."

"I don't quite follow you," Lucky says.

"I'm a sales and marketing executive, "Hyena says. "My job is to make animals *un*happy. You see, Lucky, happy animals are not good for business.

"*Un*happy animals, on the other hand, are great for business. Unhappiness gives them an empty feeling. Spending money makes the emptiness go away. That's where we come in. If we can create the unhappiness while also supplying the fix, the money comes our way.

"My marketing campaigns are designed to remove any contentment and to make animals realize they are imperfect. I let them feel they don't have enough," Hyena continues.

"Hippo used to be fine with who he was, until our weight loss ad campaign took to the printed media. After seeing our ads, Hippo became very self-conscious and unhappy about his weight. We purposefully made him unhappy with what he is, so he now mostly hides below water during the day. Our client makes a fortune selling anything from low GI grass to metabolism-boosting grass replacement tablets to him.

"Crocodile was perfectly happy with his roughly textured skin. He now applies moisturizing cream daily after seeing the ad campaign developed for one of our clients in the cosmetics industry. The cream, however, makes his skin soft and vulnerable to damage by prey and parasites. Crocodile now calls in sick for work almost twice a week. His once happy life has turned into a downward spiral.

"Zebra had the most beautiful girlfriend in the valley. That was until he saw pictures of a mare from Serengeti in a glossy wildlife magazine and became totally smitten with her. He then neglected the relationship with his girlfriend, which led to their breakup.

"The same Lion who sent you here," Hyena begins to whisper, "and please don't tell him this, but that same Lion thought he had the most beautiful mane until he saw our ads for anti-dandruff shampoo. My client is now making a killing out of sales to Lion every week."

Lucky slowly puts his hand into his pocket, retrieves the tuft of Lion's mane, and drops it to the ground unnoticed. "I'll take my chances," he whispers to himself.

"What was that?" Hyena asks.

"Nothing, "Lucky says. "It's all starting to make sense now! Since my children started watching Tom and Jerry, we've had to import cheese. No self-respecting mouse or rat even likes cheese! But Jerry loved cheese, and because he was their hero, it meant my children also had to have cheese."

"That's right down our alley," Hyena says. "It doesn't even have to be an ad or marketing material. Something as innocent as a story for children will also do the trick. The media is very powerful and it's here to stay.

"My advice is to be happy with the fur you live in, despite any shortcomings you may have," Hyena says. "You're not perfect, but then again, nobody is. You should work on your weaknesses and accept your shortcomings, but never ever become morally unhappy because of them."

"Thanks, Hyena, you have given me quite an interesting perspective on happiness," Lucky says. "I suppose it sometimes takes a crook to catch a crook?"

With these words, the two of them head their separate ways until Hyena's laughter fades away in the distance.

7

Baboon's Formula for Happiness

The frantic bark of a baboon sentry sends the troop scuttling for the trees. Lucky wastes no time in following their lead. He heads up a giant leadwood tree and ends up on a branch next to a baboon.

Almost unaware of each other's presence, they scan the area below in search of the danger they were warned about. The grass below opens up and a leopard appears out of nowhere. He nonchalantly glances up at them but continues to walk past their tree.

"He's not on the hunt; he's just taking a stroll." Baboon shares his assessment of the situation.

"That's comforting. I still have a long way to go before sunset, so can we go down now?" Lucky asks Baboon who seems quite knowledgeable about these types of situations.

"I wouldn't go down just yet. Leopards are opportunists. It's better to wait for a safe distance to develop between him and us, and then … to wait a bit longer."

"Well, seeing as we'll be sharing a branch for some time then, my name is Lucky. I'm a math teacher, and Lion has sent me to find out all I can about happiness."

"Pleased to meet you. I am Baboon. I used to be a stuntman but hurt my back filming a series for Animal Planet. I then enrolled for a degree in animal behavior at the University of the Bushveld, but quit three years into my course. Nowadays I'm into motivational speaking so I find your mission quite intriguing.

"Are you searching for *high levels* of happiness or simply a *big amount* of happiness?" Baboon asks.

"Huh? I have no idea what you're talking about, Baboon," Lucky says after pausing for a bit.

"In that case, do you mind if I practice my upcoming presentation on exactly that topic on you? I'm presenting at the upcoming Polar Species Relocation Summit, and I sure could use a practice run in front of an audience. We can't go anywhere with the leopard still so close, and since you want to learn about the topic, we'll be helping each other out."

"I'm all ears," Lucky replies while making himself comfortable on the branch.

"The essence of my presentation is much easier to explain using a picture. Take a good look at the graph on this leaf from a coral tree," Baboon says as he neatly unfolds the leaf and presents it to Lucky.

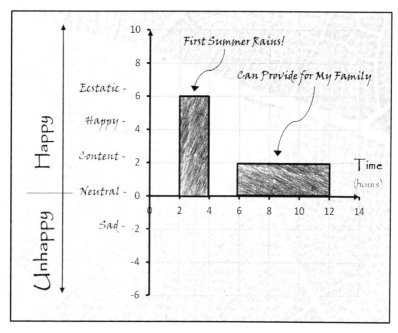

Leaf 7.1 – Level of Happiness vs. Amount of Happiness

"I have plotted two happy events on the graph. During the first event, the first summer rains last for two hours. The rain makes us ecstatic, so it scores a six on the vertical axis of the graph.

"During the second event, an animal feels content about his steady job and knowing he can provide for his family. This feeling only scores a two on the vertical axis, but it lasts, for argument's sake, for six hours.

"Now here is the interesting part. One event reaches ecstasy and the other only a level of contentment, yet both of them contain exactly the same *amount* of happiness. The size of the rectangles representing these events is the same; hence, the same *amount* of happiness.

"Just to prove my point, the math is as follows," Baboon continues. "For the first summer rains, the *amount* of happiness is calculated as:

Level 6 (ecstatic) × 2 hours = 12 happiness hours

"For knowing we can provide for our families, the *amount* of happiness is calculated as:

Level 2 (content) × 6 hours = 12 happiness hours

"So there you have proof that both rectangles indeed have the same size; therefore, both events contain the same amount of happiness," Baboon concludes.

"This is amazing stuff!" Lucky says with excitement.

"It is, isn't it," Baboon concurs. "Society places a strong emphasis on events having high levels of happiness, like the ecstasy during the first summer rains. We mostly search for happiness highs. We search for adrenalin-rush-type events that give high *levels* of happiness. We seek instant gratification, unwilling to wait for happiness to accumulate with time," Baboon continues feverishly.

"We miss so much happiness when discounting the little things in life. The happiness level one and two emotions on this graph are very important. The emotions called contentment, appreciation, and gratitude are not adrenalin-filled emotions, but with the duration of a lifetime, they could give us a rectangle dwarfing the highest of highs.

"Being content for a year will give you 2 (level) x 5,840 waking hours = 11,680 happiness hours. To get this same *amount* of happiness from being ecstatic, one would have to be ecstatic for almost 2,000 hours or 120 days in the year, which is a tall order.

"Do you know the best part about the level one and two emotions, Lucky?" Baboon says in a much calmer voice. "They don't cost a thing. They just require a conscious thought every now and again.

"The instant gratification events to achieve happiness levels of nine or ten on the other hand can be expensive. It may be a shopping spree, a new car, or a weekend getaway, but these events are generally costly with happiness of a more temporary nature.

"Humans are the worst when it comes to this instant gratification. Some of them abuse drugs and other substances to satisfy their craving for a happiness level of nine or ten. They might get the desired effect at a premium price but the highs will be short lived.

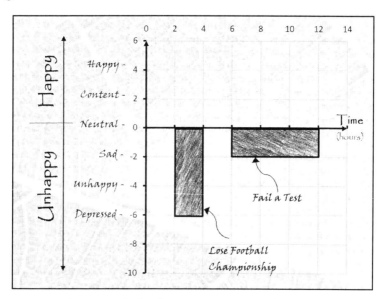

Leaf 7.2 – Level of Unhappiness vs. Amount of Unhappiness

"The opposite is also true," Baboon continues.

"We've only talked about happiness thus far. We can have the same two rectangles below the horizontal axis, which then represent *un*happy events.

"The first event could be one of severe despair at minus six, something like losing to the Carnivores in the annual Herbivore vs. Carnivore Football Championships. The other event could be a feeling of sadness when flunking a midterm test with a happiness level of only minus two.

"Similar to the happy events, both of these events contain the same amount of *un*happiness. Unhappy events with a low score, such as guilt, regret, jealousy, and failure, can contribute a great deal to leading an unhappy life, if we let them reign for long. They will give us a very big *un*happiness rectangle.

"Never underestimate the potential that lies in these low-scoring, unhappy events. They can make you just as unhappy, if not more, than a shorter but severely unhappy event."

"The stunt industry's loss is definitely a gain for the motivational-speaking fraternity," Lucky says to Baboon. "I have learned a great deal from you that I hope to pass on to Lion, and anyone else who will listen."

"You do that, Lucky. Please tell Lion to stop worrying about not being happy all the time. He only fosters those low-scoring, unhappy emotions that will rob him of happiness in the long run."

As baboon finishes these words, they notice members of the troop climbing down from the trees. Lucky and his new friend say their good-byes and continue on their separate ways as night begins to fall.

8

Honey Badger Looks Forward

"I couldn't help overhearing the last bit of your conversation with Baboon. Clever fellow, that Baboon. I have attended a few of his presentations on happiness. You need some motivation when you work as a travel agent, you know.

"Can you imagine arranging holidays for others, but never being allowed to take a holiday yourself? It's enough to get depressed about, so my employer insists we attend Baboon's presentations at the end of each rainy season. It's part of our Animal Welfare Program at work."

Lucky looks at the furry animal in front of him. "My name is Lucky, which you have probably gathered from eavesdropping on us. Who might you be?"

"I'm sorry. I am Honey Badger, travel agent extraordinaire. I arrange some pretty special holidays for my clients, you know. I'm probably best known for arranging the Great Wildebeest Migration every year. There are a lot of logistics involved as I'm sure you can imagine.

"My specialty, however, is my Big Five Holiday package," Honey Badger continues as he looks to make a sale. "We guarantee seeing humans from the five biggest continents during these trips.

"The package includes four nights' accommodations in a luxury game park, which by the way is guaranteed to be poacher free. We parade the humans past your own private patch of shade on a special viewing vehicle that resembles a sports stand. You don't even have to break a sweat to see them.

"We seldom get humans from Antarctica though. It's the fifth-largest continent, so technically the package isn't really the Big Five. But the Big Five phrase is so catchy and no one gets hurt in the process, so no harm done, I suppose."

"I'm not really interested in travel packages," Lucky interrupts. "My interest is happiness. Can you share anything new that Baboon hasn't already told me?"

"I definitely can," Honey Badger replies. "If we want more happiness, we want to increase our *amount* of happiness, am I right?"

"Yes you are," Lucky replies.

"Now there is a formula for calculating the *amount* of happiness," Honey Badger continues. "You may have gathered this from your discussion with Baboon. Simplified, the formula looks like this." Honey Badger scribbles on the leaf of a coral tree:

Happiness Amount (HA) = Happiness Level (HL) x Happiness Duration (HD), or simply :

HA = HL x HD

"This formula shows that our happiness (HA) depends on *how happy* (HL) we are and *how long* (HD) we experience that happiness.

"Looking at the formula then, we need to increase HL or HD, or both, if we want to increase HA and have more happiness," Honey Badger says.

"We're all pretty good at increasing our happiness levels (HL). It's sadly not the case for our happiness duration (HD). We can increase our happiness durations simply by planning more happy events into our lives."

"But we do plan for holidays and other happy events in our lives," Lucky says with a puzzled look on his face.

"We do, but we think the event itself will be the only happiness. By doing this, we lose out on the happiness of looking forward to the event," Honey Badger replies.

"Let's presume you have booked a seventy-two-hour Caribbean cruise for you and your family. It has been booked a year in advance.

"Let's now say you daydream about the cruise, the relaxation, and the cheese buffets for five minutes every day. If you do this for three hundred sixty-five days in the run up to the trip, you accumulate thirty hours of happy time. Looking forward to the trip effectively gave you thirty hours of happiness.

"After bagging this thirty hours of happy time, the big day finally arrives and you embark on the seventy-two-hour cruise. However, things take a turn for the worse. You get seasick, and it rains continuously. You have seen all of the magician's tricks before, but, worst of all, the bikini bombshell from the brochure never got aboard the ship!

"With all these eventualities, let's assume you're only happy for fifty percent of your waking hours. This equates to only twenty-four hours of *actual* happy time during your cruise.

"Comparing the twenty-four happy hours of the trip to the thirty happy hours you got from looking forward to the trip illustrates my point. Looking forward to something can make you happier than the event itself.

"Incidentally," Honey Badger adds, "if you only booked the trip twenty-four days in advance, you would only get two hours of happy time looking forward to the trip. Scheduling fun things well in advance helps to maximize your happiness."

"That's quite an insightful comparison, Honey Badger," Lucky says.

"It certainly is," Honey Badger replies. "Some assumptions are quite conservative to illustrate my point, but I'm sure you get the gist of this comparison. If you plan happiness into your life, chances are good that you *will* be happy.

"To-do lists, on the other hand, mostly plan *un*happiness into our lives. These lists gravitate more toward being *have*-to-do lists than *want*-to-do lists. Though sometimes essential, *have*-to-do lists contain things we want to get out of the way. We generally don't look forward to doing things on the list.

"If we spend just as much time compiling *want*-to-do lists, we have a visual reminder of things to look forward to with the happiness that it brings," Honey Badger concludes.

"Thanks for this extraordinary explanation," Lucky says.

"The pleasure is all mine," Honey Badger says. "Here, take one of my business cards. If you have a holiday on your want-to-do list, you know who to call."

9

The Journey of a Baobab Tree

The sun has reached its highest point. Lucky scuffles along at a sluggish pace. He hasn't eaten for a while, and the sweltering heat is tapping his reserves.

"City life is easy," Lucky thinks. "I now understand why they call them convenience stores."

Lucky notices a giant baobab tree and eagerly heads for the shade it offers. After reaching the tree, he frantically scratches around for food in the pockets formed by the intermingling roots. With the menu at three insects and a mushroom, a voice from above interrupts him.

"What are you looking for?"

Almost intuitively, Lucky responds, "Happiness. I'm looking for advice on happiness."

"You won't find it in there, that's for sure!" the voice responds. Before Lucky can explain himself, the introduction follows. "Hi there! Did not mean to frighten you. I am Baobab."

The eventual realization that a tree is talking to him stifles any hunger pains Lucky still had. "My name is Lucky," he replies. "What I meant to say was that Lion sent me on a fact-finding mission on happiness."

"Not sure I can help you there," Baobab replies. "I'm into carbon credit trading. Been doing it since the days when green was just a color. It must be getting close to twelve rainy seasons now."

"Don't sell yourself short," Lucky says. "I have already come across a surgeon and a landscape architect who gave me great insights into happiness. Neither of them worked in the field of emotional sciences, so even you could have a story to share."

"Why didn't you say so? Stories I can help you with," Baobab says.

"Ever since my days as a sapling," Baobab starts, "I wanted to be the biggest tree in the Bushveld. I wanted to be the first to see what lies outside this valley. Life becomes very dull when you see the same hilltops day in, day out, year after year. You won't believe how frustrating it is being stuck in one spot without the pleasure of traveling the world.

"My whole life revolved around achieving this goal. I also reasoned I would become smarter than other trees, if I could see what they couldn't. Being smarter would earn me their respect and admiration. I believed I would get permanent happiness if others idolized me. In essence, I believed I would be happy once I could see outside the valley.

"I needed to be tall to see outside the valley. To be tall enough, I had to accelerate my growing. I absorbed my minerals six times a day and took deep breaths of carbon dioxide whenever animals were around.

"When the sun's first rays hit me, I photosynthesized like there was no tomorrow. I pushed my roots deeper every day. I pushed them down to where no tree has ever gone in search of water.

"Then, it finally happened two rainy seasons ago. I caught my first glimpse of the outside world. At first, I was ecstatic, and I shared the views from afar with those around me. I received some admiration and even a bit more respect, but the permanent state of happiness I longed for never came.

"Life continued as before. The wind, rain, and sun continued to make me happy. Droughts, wildfires, and lightning still made me *unhappy*. My ability to see outside the valley didn't make these unhappy events disappear.

"Come to think of it, I'm somewhat of a sadder tree after achieving my lifelong goal.

"Realizing I spent half my life chasing a permanent state of happiness that never existed filled me with regret. I made my happiness conditional on achieving something great in life. In this process, I overlooked the happiness I already had.

"I was so consumed by my goal that I missed my saplings growing up. I missed the day they broke ground and the day they got their first leaves. I was deaf to the sound of their laughter when the ants tickled their bark. I missed all these happy moments while waiting for a happiness that never came."

"It must be terrible living with such regret," Lucky responds.

"It was initially, but half my life is left. I have realized my mistake and now treasure the little bits of happiness in every day.

"I fear many of us are falling in the same trap I did. They think they will be happy when they reach a milestone. Happy when they get that promotion. Happy when they reach their goal weight. Happy when they have lots of money.

"Anyone able to complete the sentence 'I will be happy when …' is in the same trap I was and losing out on everyday happiness. Tell this to Lion. He is still young and must not make the same mistake I did."

"I will tell your story to Lion," Lucky says. "I also want to thank you, as I have personally gained a lot from your story. I thought I would be happy when I retired. I do love teaching, but it consumes so much free time.

"Retirement would give me the free time and associated happiness I crave. At least I used to think so. I was heading down the same path you were on. Thanks to your advice I can now make a change."

As the shadows in the Bushveld turn into dawn, Lucky tells his friend of a world outside the valley. Of life in the city and places far beyond the valley that is Baobab's world.

10

In the Head of an Impala

At the break of dawn, Lucky heads into a blanket of early morning mist enveloping the Bushveld. He pushes forward in spite of poor visibility. His ears and nose are now the primary senses for locating animals that can help him in his quest.

Twenty minutes into the mist, Lucky faintly hears the snorting of impala in the distance. Cautiously, he changes direction toward the antelopes. He is all too aware that snorting is their high-alert call when predators lurk nearby.

The intermittent snorting grows louder. As if from nowhere, the silhouette of an enormous impala appears through the mist. The animal is visibly tense, but despite being on high alert, he is unaware of Lucky's presence.

So the two of them stand, Lucky looking at the Impala and the Impala staring into the mist with his head tilted slightly upward. Minutes pass by until Lucky cannot bear the tension of the deadly silence any longer.

"Are we on the menu?" Lucky whispers in a tone meant to startle as little as possible.

As if waking up from a dream, Impala slowly turns his head toward Lucky and mumbles, "Menu?"

"Predators!" Lucky whispers as loudly as he dares. "Have you seen or heard predators that see us as their breakfast?"

"Not at all," Impala says. "Whatever gave you that idea, and why do you interrupt my meditation?"

"Meditation?" Lucky asks. "I thought you were sensing predators. You seemed so focused and in the zone the way you stood there. I have seen how you guys do it on Animal Planet."

"You must be a city rat," Impala mumbles to himself. "You heard right about the meditation. That's what any good animal psychologist does from time to time."

"Then you must be an expert on happiness," Lucky responds with enthusiasm and expands on the details of his mission.

"Now that's ironic." Impala chuckles loudly. "Lion and his wives make us live in fear. They show no mercy when hunting us. They are the main reason for the herd being unhappy, yet he wants to learn from us about happiness?

"Despite the sentiment, I'll help you to help Lion," Impala says. "There is no sense in trying to upset the food chain here, but you *must* put in a good word for us in return. Lion and his family should really get more of the *other* antelope species into their diet and give us a break."

"I'll convey your request, but that's all I can promise," Lucky says. "Your species unfortunately ranks quite high on Lion's list of delicacies."

"I suppose I can't ask for more, so here is my story," Impala says.

"As you can imagine, being an impala is extremely stressful. Our sole purpose in life is to stand around waiting for lions or other predators to eat us. We constantly live on the borderline of depression, so trying to be happy takes quite a concerted effort.

"We've tried herbal medicines and even root beer to lift our spirits, but had no success. We've even placed ads in the *Bushveld Times*, highlighting the health risks associated with our red meat. No success there either. Either predators can't read, or they are not concerned about their health. Nothing we tried took away our stress or gave us happiness.

"Have you ever seen an impala smile, Lucky?" Impala asks. After a brief moment of silence, he says, "I didn't think so, but now at least you know why."

"All of the impala in our herd suffered from predator-induced anxiety syndrome. With no known treatment, I established a support group so we could at least share our fears and anxieties.

"In our support group, we try to lighten our loads based on a theory I developed. My theory is that one can be happy despite living in unhappy surroundings. For us it means we can be happy regardless of the constant fear of predators."

"It sounds simple enough," Lucky interrupts, full of skepticism. "Have you ever tested this theory of yours?"

"Let me put it to you this way," Impala says. "If I asked you where you lived, what would you reply?"

"I would say I lived in my den at Forty-Four Acacia Avenue," Lucky says.

"That may be the place where you *reside*, Lucky, but it's not the place you *live*," Impala replies with somewhat of a grin.

Lucky looks dumfounded but realizes Impala is on to something.

"You live in your head, Lucky, just like all of us. Our emotions, such as happiness, are determined by our thoughts rather than our surroundings.

"Have you ever been in a bad situation, but managed to have happy thoughts regardless of the bad situation?" Impala asks.

"Yes, I have," Lucky says after thinking for a while. "Every morning I get stuck in the rush-hour stampede on my way to work. It's quite stressful and frustrating, but my thoughts often wander to a recent family holiday, or I listen to my favorite music. That lifts my spirit despite the rush-hour stampede."

"Exactly!" Impala replies with excitement. "We can only have one thought at a time. That one thought can be either happy or unhappy. We have the power to decide which one it will be, regardless of our circumstances. Happy thoughts can therefore make us happy despite being in unhappy surroundings.

"Unfortunately the opposite is also true," Impala continues. "You could be in a happy environment, like the family holiday you mentioned. However, if you constantly worry about work, you will be *unhappy,* regardless of your happy surroundings.

"Similarly, playing with your kids in their hamster wheel will be less enjoyable if you're already thinking about tomorrow's rush-hour stampede.

"The key to all of this is your ability to control the world you *live* in. You must choose your thoughts carefully. Sometimes you should consciously stop your thoughts wandering down a path of unhappiness. Replacing negative thoughts with positive ones is key to living in a happy world."

"What a simple but effective technique," Lucky says. "But surely having predators lurking at night is a lot worse than my rush-hour stampede? Does this technique help the herd to lead happy lives?"

"Yes, it does," Impala replies confidently. "We have a choice at night. We can think about lions lurking in the dark and be unhappy all the time. However, we purposefully think about something nice, like starring on Animal Planet, to make us feel happy.

"We even got ourselves a television. Why do you think television is so popular in our modern, stressful life?" Impala asks. "The television actually functions as a thought generator. Pleasant thoughts, from watching something nice, replace any unhappy thoughts we may have since we can only have one thought at any given time."

"You have really been a great help, Impala," Lucky says. "The mist has cleared so I'll be on my way again. I'll remember your advice and also put in a good word for you with Lion."

11

Dung Beetle for a Change

Lucky wakes up to the majestic call of a fish eagle who triumphantly announces his catch to the entire Bushveld. Lucky slowly lifts his head to survey his surroundings.

"Wonder which way I should head today," he thinks.

While pondering his next move, Lucky spots movement in the short grass not far from him. He gets up for a better look and sees a beetle rolling a ball through the grass.

"This can't be football or rugby," Lucky thinks. "The beetle is all alone and his technique all wrong."

Lucky takes a closer look at the beetle. The beetle is in a handstand position. He supports his weight on his front legs, while rolling and manipulating the ball with his hind legs.

"What sport are you practicing there?" Lucky asks, after curiosity eventually gets the better of him.

The ball stops rolling. The beetle turns around, climbs on top of the ball, and looks straight at Lucky.

"It's not a sport; it's my job," the beetle says, annoyed. "I'm a waste recycling expert. I'm rolling this fresh ball of nutrient-rich dung to a spot in need of fertilization."

"My name is Lucky, and I'm a rat on a mission," he responds, not wanting to sound less important.

"Pleasure to meet you. I am Dung Beetle. Is your mission also along the lines of fertilization?"

"Fertilization of the mind, I suppose," Lucky replies. "I'm actually here at the request of Lion. He wants to know what makes different animals happy."

"What animals are you looking for?" Dung Beetle asks.

"Animals like you. In fact, any animal with a story or lesson about happiness."

"Well, I suppose recycling can be put on hold for a while to attend to Lion's request," Dung Beetle replies. He gets onto his hind legs on top of his ball as if to address an audience.

"You asked about sport earlier. Well, I'm a bodybuilder," Dung Beetle proudly announces as he flexes his pecks.

"Rolling balls of dung every day gave my upper body great muscle definition. You can imagine what supporting your entire body weight on your front legs will do for you. Moving into bodybuilding was the logical next step for me.

"I began entering competitions but always finished third or fourth in the Annual Bushveld Bodybuilding Competition (ABBC). I had to do something different. I started rolling elephant and rhino dung exclusively. These were heavier than what I normally used. This had the desired effect. My torso grew bigger and sported even greater muscle definition.

"In spite of all these extra efforts, I still couldn't win the ABBC. Each year I managed a commendable second place. Guerilla, who travels all the way from Central Africa to compete, took top honors every year.

"One day, after yet another second place, I swallowed my pride and approached an ABBC judge for advice after the competition. I still remember him saying, 'Your hind legs are pathetic!' However cruel those words were, it changed my life for the better.

"I now had to find time to exercise my hind legs every day. Rolling dung, however is a full-time job. After work, my family and chores at home demanded my attention. By the time all the have-to-dos of the day were done, I hit the bed for an early start. Those herbivores don't stop producing dung just because a beetle wants to get some sleep you know.

"Finding extra time in the morning was impossible. I already had to get up early to catch up on all the nighttime deposits.

"I soon realized I could only exercise my hind legs while I was working. My hind legs had to do what my front legs had been doing up to that point.

"I changed my dung-rolling technique. Now, I stood up straight and supported my body weight on my *hind* legs. While leaning against the dung ball with my upper body, my hind legs propelled the dung ball forward.

"Such a technique was unprecedented for dung beetles. I had deviated from a technique that dated back even further than the Big Cleanup my ancestors performed on Noah's Ark.

"The new technique was difficult in those early days. I couldn't get out of bed the first day. My hind legs were aching like you wouldn't believe. However, I persevered with the technique, and after eight full moons, I had the muscular hind legs to complement my upper body. I have won the ABBC ever since.

"I would never have won the competition if I didn't change my technique. I had to do something different in order to get a different result.

"The same principle applies to happiness, Lucky," Dung Beetle continues. "Something only makes you happy for so long. After a while, you get used to that something and it doesn't give you the joy it used to.

"From time to time, we need to do different things, or we need to do the same things differently. It has been said that doing what you have always done will give you what you have always gotten."

"I know exactly what you mean, my genius friend!" Lucky replies, excitedly. "Math and teaching have always been my passion. Over the years, however, teaching turned into something I had to do to make a living. The joy and the passion it used to give me had gradually disappeared.

"When Lion asked me to travel his kingdom, it brought the change I needed. Doing something different gave me a new passion for life. I'm also looking forward to teaching again after I get back home."

"I'm glad you came to that realization," Dung Beetle says. "You have to excuse me, however, as I feel my muscles getting stiff. I need to keep them moving, so I must head on out."

"I understand," Lucky replies as he watches the beetle and his ball disappear into the long grass.

12

Butterfly's Unhappy Metamorphosis

Lucky heads for a grove of sickle bush trees in search of food. He notices a magnificent black and yellow butterfly flying in the same direction.

"Any idea where a rat can get a bite to eat around here?" Lucky asks.

"Sure I do; just follow my lead. I am Butterfly, by the way. You might know me as the current Miss Animal Kingdom."

Lucky, who has now caught up with Butterfly, examines her from antennae to tail, trying to recognize her. "You're very beautiful, but I must admit I don't really follow beauty pageants. My name is Lucky. I have been tasked by Lion to find out all there is to know about happiness."

"I can help you!" Butterfly responds without hesitation. "I'm not just a pretty wing, you know."

"I need all the help I can get, and I would really appreciate if you shared your story with me," Lucky says.

"I need to ask you something first, Lucky," Butterfly says. "What's the earliest memory you have in life?"

"Mm, I think it was when I got a calculator for my third birthday," Lucky responds.

"Well, my earliest memory comes from my days as an embryo. I was tucked away in my egg among my brothers and sisters on the leaf of a monkey thorn tree. I still remember seeing caterpillars through the thin shell of my egg,"

Butterfly says.

"The caterpillars wandered somewhat aimlessly on the surrounding leaves, sometimes chewing on them as they went along. I remember how divine those juicy leaves looked. I was fed up surviving on egg yolk in my claustrophobic prison. I couldn't wait to hatch as a caterpillar so I could stretch my forty-eight legs and roam free to eat anything but egg yolk.

"The big day finally arrived. Early one spring morning, I hatched, and though my legs were still shaky, I soon crawled all over the branch where I was born. I stuffed my mouth with leaves as I went along. Life as a caterpillar was great.

"I soon realized, however, that a caterpillar was appetizing to many animals that were out and about. I didn't have the safety of my eggshell any more. Munching on leaves also started losing its appeal after a few days. The life of a caterpillar that I once envied so much was suddenly not so great anymore.

"One day, however, I saw a butterfly flying from flower to flower. It was the most beautiful creature I had ever seen. Life as a butterfly seemed so carefree and full of fun.

"From that day onward I couldn't wait to become a butterfly. I despised every moment of being a caterpillar. Why eat leaves and be ugly when you can live on nectar and be beautiful?

"And then, finally, after twelve agonizing days, I emerged from my cocoon as a butterfly. I was ready to start living life! I frequented all the flowers in the neighborhood and drank nectar until my stomach felt like bursting.

"Life as a butterfly was truly great, but soon I realized that butterflies were even more conspicuous than caterpillars. I was in real danger of becoming a meal for another animal. I also realized that butterflies compete with bees for nectar and that Nature gave us nothing to rival their stingers.

"The hassles of a butterfly don't stop there though! The Bushveld Aviation Authority requires all flying insects to submit flight plans to safeguard them against spiderwebs.

"So here I am, a butterfly at last, with only a few days left to find a mate and lay my eggs. Soon I will complete the circle of life and die.

"I have no fear of death. What robs me of my happiness is the deep regret I have for wishing my life away. I was never content with the phase of life I was in, nor did I reap any happiness from it. I always saw happiness in the next phase of my life. I continued to postpone my happiness.

"Therefore my advice is to enjoy each phase of life for what it is. Your childhood, working life, and years of retirement all have happiness to offer.

"Focus on the positive aspects of each phase, so you can reap happiness from it. Accept the negatives and deal with it. The next phase in your life will also have negatives to deal with, so thinking you will be happy then is a fallacy."

"You're definitely not just a pretty wing," Lucky says, clearing a lump from his throat. "I hope you find your mate and have an abundance of happiness in your remaining days."

With these words, the two of them part ways. Butterfly flies off to search for nectar, while Lucky continues searching for something to eat.

13

The Fish Eagle in the Hammock

It is a scorching hot day in the African Bushveld. Lucky kneels on the bank of the Limpopo River to quench his thirst when a voice from above says, "Say, aren't you the guy who wrote that book on surviving global warming?"

"That would be me," Lucky responds. He looks up to see Fish Eagle perched on a dry branch above him.

"But what about us?" Fish Eagle asks, showing no emotion in his piercing eyes.

"I don't quite follow you," Lucky says.

"What about the non-mammals and the winged ones like me? You only covered survival techniques for *wingless mammals* in your book. Are we supposed to circle the rising waters for eternity?"

"I haven't really thought about it, not being a bird myself. Why don't *you* write such a book? You seem pretty well qualified for that."

"I can't write. I'm a simple creature. I live off what the river provides," Fish Eagle says. He then retreats to his nearby hammock overlooking the Limpopo River.

"So you catch fish for a living then?" Lucky asks.

"Pretty much yes, but I don't catch fish all day long. I only need a couple of fish to survive. It takes me an hour or so every day to catch them. I spend the rest of my time in this hammock. I take in the beautiful view while lying in the shade of this tree."

"I think I can help you," Lucky responds.

"Help me?" Fish Eagle curiously asks.

"Yes, help you. I need to teach you the principles of good business. How much fish is out there?"

"There is probably more than I could ever catch in a hundred lifetimes," Fish Eagle says.

"Great! Now here is what you must do," Lucky says. "Every day, you need to catch more fish than you need. It will be hard work initially, but it's important to catch as many fish as you can."

"And what am I supposed to do with all that fish? I can only eat so many, and the rest will go to waste."

"You sell them at the market. Pretty soon you will have enough money to buy fishing nets," Lucky says.

"And why do I need fishing nets? I have already told you I have as much fish as I can possibly eat."

"You need them to catch even more fish, of course! If you have more nets, you will catch more fish, so you can make more money selling them at the market. Pretty soon you will be able to buy a small boat."

"And why do I need a boat?"

"To get to where the big shoals of fish are and to allow faster deployment of your nets," Lucky replies. He is excited to share his knowledge in guiding Fish Eagle toward a better life.

"With your boat, you will catch even more fish. You'll make even more money and pretty soon you can afford a fair-sized fishing trawler."

"And I guess I need the fishing trawler to catch even more fish?" Fish Eagle replies.

"Now you're talking!" Lucky says. His pupil is finally beginning to understand the principles of good business.

"With this trawler, you can catch more fish than you ever dreamed of. You can register a company and deduct some expenses from your taxes. Before long, you can buy more trawlers and control the entire fishing industry of this area. You can build a warehouse stacked with freezers that will help exporting fish to neighboring countries. Hundreds of animals will be working for you."

"And why on earth do I want all of that?" Fish Eagle says.

"To make more money. Lots of it!" Lucky feverishly replies.

"And what am I supposed to do with all that money?" Fish Eagle asks.

"You can use the money to appoint a manager for your business. This will give you the time, on top of your money, to enjoy life to the fullest. The manager will free you up to spend your time in the shade of a tree with nothing to do but stare across the river."

Fish Eagle grins and stretches out in his hammock.

"I'm already there," Fish Eagle replies as he stares across the river. "Sometimes, Lucky, the happiness we search for is already there. We only need to see it, to enjoy it."

14

Beaver Working Smartly

Without much warning, a large African teak tree crashes to the ground and silences the birds that were announcing a new day in the Bushveld. Lucky heads to the ruckus to see what the fuss is about.

He cautiously approaches the fallen giant and sees a strange-looking animal on the trunk of the slain tree.

"The name is Beaver," the animal introduces himself with a sense of accomplishment.

"My name is Lucky" comes the reply. "And what brings you to Africa?"

"I'm in the import and export business. Timber to be precise," Beaver says. "Activists caused so much uproar about deforestation in the Amazon that I had to source my timber outside of the Americas. My search for timber that grows below the radar has led me all the way to Africa."

"So it is timber that makes you happy then, Beaver?" Lucky fires away. Feedback from international respondents will add considerable weight to his findings.

"Why are you asking?" Beaver says. Lucky elaborates about his quest.

"You're clearly not a businessman, are you?" Beaver says. Before Lucky can respond, Beaver continues, "There is no such thing as a free lunch, Lucky. Free advice in the world of business doesn't exist. You will have to *earn* my advice."

"And how do I go about doing that?" Lucky asks.

"I have clients," Beaver starts. "A flock of urbanized woodpeckers from the north are breathing down my neck for timber. I should have delivered to them already, but I'm behind on production. I really could use an extra pair of paws."

"I'm a math teacher, so I can help with your financial reconciliations," Lucky says, trying to change the direction of the discussion.

"They are up to date," Beaver says abruptly. "I need you to swing an ax, Lucky. You must help me cut down these trees." He points to the forest in front of them.

"I'll make you a deal," Beaver says as he picks up his ax. "If you fell more trees than I do by sunset, I'll pay for your time *and* give you my take on happiness. However, if I win, you still get the advice but not the money. Do we have a deal or not?"

Lucky surveys Beaver from head to toe for something to indicate whether he should accept the challenge or not. The plump figure in front of him has an odd-looking tail and teeth that would occupy an orthodontist for months. Beaver definitely does not fit his image of a good lumberjack, so Lucky picks up his ax and replies, "We have a deal."

With an unceremonious "Go!" from Beaver, they attack the first trees they can find. Trees topple over throughout the morning as Lucky and Beaver compete for victory.

They remain neck and neck as their blows continue to echo through the forest. Finally, with the sun reaching its best vantage point, the forest falls silent again with both animals breaking for lunch.

After his lunch, Lucky stuffs a last fistful of berries into his mouth, picks up his ax, and sets off again.

With each blow of his ax, Lucky's grin grows wider as he sees his lead increase. As Lucky's first tree after the lunch break falls, Beaver is still nowhere to be seen or heard.

Beaver finally appears ten minutes later. Lucky is about to start on his third tree after returning from lunch. Their eyes briefly meet. Beaver then lifts his ax and starts his afternoon session.

So they continue, relentlessly wielding their axes and stopping only to wipe the sweat from their eyes. The sun finally calls it a day, and the long tree shadows announce the onset of night.

"Stop!" comes the instruction from Beaver as he ends their shift for the day.

"How many?" Lucky pants as he struggles for air.

"Twenty-four," Beaver replies.

"Impossible!" Lucky exclaims. "I have one less at twenty-three. And that after you took a long and extended lunch," Lucky says. His eyes interrogate Beaver's face for a sign that he's not being truthful.

"Twenty-four," Beaver replies again.

"You're a reasonable lumberjack, but counting isn't one of your strengths," Lucky mutters as he sets off to count Beaver's tally.

Lucky returns a few minutes later and barely makes eye contact with Beaver. "And what is thy verdict, oh numerical one?" Beaver inquires as Lucky approaches him.

"Twenty-four," Lucky replies. His voice is barely audible amid the soft rustling of the leaves.

"What a strange coincidence," Beaver says. "After counting them initially, I came to exactly …"

"Okay, okay!" Lucky interrupts him. "You win. I just can't understand how you beat me having wasted thirty minutes after lunch. You could have cut down trees in that time, but you wasted it instead."

"I wasn't wasting time, Lucky. I actually spent that time quite wisely."

"Wisely?" Lucky asks.

"Yes," Beaver replies. "After you left our lunch spot, I spent twenty minutes resting in order to regain my strength for the afternoon."

"And the other ten minutes?" Lucky asks.

"The other ten minutes were spent sharpening the blade of my ax," Beaver replies. "Anyway, thanks for all your help, Lucky. I'm an animal of my word. I will share my advice on happiness with you as agreed. Having lived through today, you probably know what the advice is already."

"I have a good idea," Lucky says. "But I wouldn't mind hearing it from you. After all, I have spent the whole day felling trees just to hear this advice."

"Take life slower," Beaver says. "You will have more time to think about what you're doing and where you're going. Working yourself to death doesn't guarantee better results. It only guarantees giving up some happiness."

"True words," Lucky says as his breathing returns to normal. "I probably won't make Lion cut down trees for this advice, but he will appreciate it nonetheless."

After a shake of the paws, the foreign businessman with his haul of trees and the math teacher on his quest for knowledge disappear into the night and head their separate ways.

15

Blessings without a Rhino's Horn

The raging wind herds big clouds together in a single dark mass covering the Bushveld. The distant sound of thunder grows louder as the wind howls across the treetops.

"I must get away from the trees so lightning doesn't fry me," Lucky thinks as he heads for a clearing in the fading light.

Roughly in the center of the clearing, he sees the silhouette of an animal unlike anything he has seen before. It looks like an adult rhino, but without the horn.

"It must be another foreigner working with Beaver in his lumber business," Lucky thinks as he approaches the animal.

"Hi there. My name is Lucky," he says. The animal stops grazing and lifts his head to see the new arrival.

"I'm Rhino," the strange-looking creature replies.

"Which part of the world are you from?" Lucky asks as his eyes lock onto the scars of an old wound on Rhino's face.

"I'm from here. I am from the Bushveld. I'm a full-blooded African black rhino," he says proudly.

Rhino then continues on a sadder note. "Don't let my blunt nose fool you. I lost my horn to human poachers one rainy season ago. I'm one of the lucky ones. They only sedated me with a dart gun before cutting off my horn. Many of my species pay with their lives before their horns are taken."

"But why would humans do that when the best place for it is clearly there where Nature put it originally?" Lucky asks.

"Some humans in Asia believe our horns have supernatural powers for men who find their mating ritual a bit strenuous. They use it as an aphrodisiac of some sorts."

Lucky bursts out laughing. "Of all the stupid things humans do, that must be the most ridiculous thing I have ever heard!"

"Ridiculous indeed, but whether it actually works for them is irrelevant. Their selfishness has left me without my horn. Left me without what defines me as a rhino."

Lucky swallows his laugh as he notices a sadness creeping into Rhino's voice.

"Isn't it funny how you never appreciate something while you still have it?" Rhino says. "You're *un*happy when you lose it, so really you should be happy while still having it.

"I suppose life doesn't work that way," he continues. "We take so many things for granted without appreciating them enough. Take you for example, Lucky. Do you count your blessings every day?" Rhino locks eyes with Lucky.

Lucky finds himself at a loss for words, partly due to the intimidating figure in front of him, but also due to the unexpectedness of such a direct question.

"In my days as a librarian, I read many books," Rhino says. "Those were the days I could still face children visiting the library, without fear of jokes behind my back about my disfigured face.

"Anyway, that's in the past. I hope that I can prevent others from making the same mistake I did. Maybe I can help them appreciate what they have, before it's too late.

"I bet there are many basics you take for granted, Lucky," Rhino says. "You're not on any endangered species list. You live in an area that frequently gets rain. You're a free-range rat and not the subject of medical trials. These are all things I'm sure you take for granted. You may not be happy that you have them, but I bet you will be very unhappy if you lose them."

"You have a very good point there, Rhino," Lucky says. "I'm researching the subject of happiness for Lion, and what you have just said has great value for my research.

"I suppose being grateful and regularly counting your blessings make you content in some way or another." As Lucky utters the words, he remembers the graph Baboon showed him.

"Baboon showed me proof for what you're saying, Rhino," Lucky says. "He had a graph explaining the difference between the *level* and the *amount* of happiness we experience."

Lucky shows Rhino a copy of Baboon's graph and continues to explain the difference between level of happiness and amount of happiness.

"Being content gives you a low level of happiness. However, your contentment is spread out over a lifetime if you regularly count your blessings. It gives you a very big rectangle on the graph, so you get a lot of happiness just by being content," Lucky says as he draws another graph in the sand.

As he once again notices the sad, disfigured face of Rhino, he remembers what Elephant taught him about a crisis. Without hesitation, he tells Elephant's story to Rhino in the hope that it will lighten his load.

"Thanks for your advice, Rhino," Lucky concludes. "I will definitely count my blessings more often. I'm sure Lion has many blessings of which he is unaware. Once he realizes this, and appreciates what he has, it will help to make him a happier animal."

"I need to thank *you*, my friend," Rhino replies. "You have given me hope, and I will look for the opportunities in my crisis."

16

More for Bush Pig

Massive drops of rain fall from the heavens. Lucky searches frantically for shelter from the storm, which is only minutes away.

He scuttles down the first burrow he finds. Protected from the rain, he sits against the entrance wall in order to catch his breath. As his breathing returns to normal, Lucky becomes aware of another animal breathing deeper down the burrow.

"Hello …?" is all that Lucky gets out in a high-pitched voice. The pace of his breathing shoots up again.

"You can stay in my home until the storm passes, friend," a voice reassures Lucky from the back of the burrow.

As his eyes get used to the darkness, Lucky makes out the figure of a piglike animal lying down calmly and looking straight at him.

Lucky introduces himself and explains the reason for his travels.

"I am Bush Pig," the figure introduces himself. "I might be able to help you in your quest, so here is my story.

"When I began practicing as a veterinarian, I used to be in it for the money," Bush Pig says. "It gave me a kick to see the money roll in, and living the high life became an obsession.

"I had a flashy burrow up in Diamond Hill. I decorated the place with fine and exquisite things. I had a plumber work the place for two weeks to install a mud-on-tap system for my hippo-sized mud bath.

"I even splashed out on additional roof supports and had the whole place damp proofed. My own botanist trimmed the roots growing into my burrow on a weekly basis.

"Very soon I had everything I wanted and more," Bush Pig continues. "The mortgage for the burrow was paid off in my first two years of practicing."

"After some time, making money no longer gave me the thrill it used to. I developed a feeling of emptiness inside. My zest and my passion for life were gone. I realized I was no longer happy, but I had no idea what to do about it.

"One ordinary day, however, Cheetah visited my practice. He had developed severe joint aches and was unable to hunt or provide for his family. I diagnosed him with a clear case of omega-3 deficiency, the type one would expect from carnivores not eating fish.

"Cheetah had no money to pay me, but I treated him nonetheless. I'm not sure why. I would never have done such a thing in my early days of practicing. Something inside me wanted to help this desperate creature at all costs.

"Cheetah was back to normal after only a few sessions and some changes to his diet. He was able to hunt and provide for his family once again.

"The look Cheetah gave me after completing our final session changed my life forever. The gratitude beamed from his eyes. Knowing that I helped him, without expecting something in return, gave me far more happiness than I ever got from my en suite mud bath or anything else I ever bought.

"It was the weirdest thing ever. In fact, I still grin whenever I think of that day. That day I learned something important. *Getting* doesn't always make you happy. *Giving* does.

"What you give doesn't have to be big or expensive. That's the best part. Have you ever noticed how giving a smile or compliment sometimes makes *you* feel better than the animal it was intended for?"

"I can't agree with your more, Bush Pig," Lucky says. "I suppose this exact same principle drew me to teaching originally. Passing my knowledge onto my students, and giving them insight into mathematics, gives me great pleasure. I can't help but smile when I see their eyes light up as they grasp a concept.

"Thanks for your story, Bush Pig," Lucky says as the sound of thunder fades. "I'll be on my way again."

"You're welcome, my friend. Just be careful when diving into a burrow next time. It may not be a friendly bush pig you find down below!"

17

Happy Being a Fig Tree

Lucky spots a rocky outcrop and heads toward it in search of insects hiding in the cracks and crevasses. A large African rock fig tree is perched on top of the rocky mound. To Lucky's disappointment, the roots of the tree have grown into almost every crack and other hiding spots for insects.

Lucky grabs hold of a root and climbs to the top of the rock mound where he hopes to find more cracks and food. Halfway up the root, Lucky halts his ascent. He is sure he heard something giggle.

As Lucky stops, so does the giggling, so he continues on his climb. He barely resumes his ascent when the giggling starts again. This time, he is sure of what he heard.

Lucky stops and shouts at the top of his voice, "What's so funny?"

"You're tickling my feet," a deep voice booms from the crest of the mound.

"Now if that was an insect speaking," Lucky thinks, "then I wonder just who will be having who for breakfast today. Unless … unless it's the fig tree." Lucky remembers how Baobab tree also spoke to him.

"Is that you speaking and laughing from up there, African Rock Fig tree?" Lucky shouts.

"It is, son. You can just call me African Fig. Most folks from around here don't call me by my birth names. Come on up so you can tell me where you came from. Trees like me are reliant on others for the latest news and gossip,

69

you know. It has been two weeks since something came this way. I'm dying to know what's happening out there!"

"That clears up that then," Lucky thinks. "Speaking trees are apparently not rare."

When Lucky reaches the top of the rock pile, he finds shade below one of African Fig's branches.

"My name is Lucky," he says. "I have been sent by Lion to travel across his kingdom. I need to find out from different animals, and trees also, if they have words of wisdom on happiness."

"Well, as you already know, my name is African Fig. I'm a professional rock climber like my father and my grandfather before him. I do have a story I can share with you on the topic of happiness, but first you need to give me news from where you came from."

Lucky spends the next forty minutes telling African Fig all he has seen and encountered on his travels. He also shares some of the lessons on happiness he has learned from other animals.

"Thanks for the update, Lucky. You have no idea how much it means to me. Now it's my turn, I suppose," African Fig says. He stretches his branches in preparation for his story.

"My grandfather told me the same story I'm about to tell you when I was still a sapling. Though parts of the story may seem far-fetched to an adult, they were no problem for the young and curious mind of a sapling.

"One day," African Fig starts, "Fig Tree looked up at the sun, with sweat dripping from his branches, and said, 'Who is the sun that he can burn down on the earth as he pleases? I wish I was the sun.'

"And so Fig Tree became the sun. He enjoyed burning down on earth with his powerful rays. One day, however, a cloud moved in front of the sun. It blocked its rays and cast a shadow on the earth. This cooled the earth, which aggravated the sun.

"'Who is this cloud?' the sun shouted, 'that he can block my rays and prevent me from scorching the earth? I wish I was the cloud so I could cast a shadow wherever it pleased me.'

"And so the sun became the cloud. He happily spent the next few days blocking the sun, casting a shadow wherever he pleased. However, the wind picked up and blew the cloud around the heavenly skies. This frustrated the cloud. He no longer controlled where he cast his shadow.

"'Who is this wind,' the cloud thundered, 'blowing me about as he pleases so that I can't cast my shadow where I want to? I wish I was the wind so I could blow the clouds about to my heart's content.'

"And so the cloud became the wind. He spent the next few days blowing the clouds about as he pleased. One day, however, the wind noticed a large rocky outcrop that didn't even budge, no matter how hard he blew. This resilience infuriated the wind, but the rocky outcrop stood its ground as if mocking the wind.

"'Who is this rocky outcrop,' the wind said furiously, 'that he can stand there as he chooses without succumbing to my might? I wish I was the rocky outcrop.'

"And so the wind became the rocky outcrop. It took great pleasure in standing around, without moving an inch, despite the best attempts of the wind.

"One day, while taunting the wind, the rocky outcrop noticed the roots of a fig tree entering its cracks. He felt the roots growing bigger every day until they eventually forced open the cracks even more. Sections of rock became dislodged by the ever-expanding roots and rolled down the outcrop as they broke off.

"'Who is this fig tree?' the rocky outcrop groveled, 'that he can reduce me to rubble using only his roots? I wish I was the fig tree!'

"And so the rocky outcrop became the fig tree. He was right back where he started: a fig tree being scorched by the sun.

"That's the end of the story, Lucky," African Fig says, "but Grandpa never stopped there. He believed the lesson was the most important part of the story.

"Grandpa taught me that those around us also have problems. They may seem to have perfect lives, but they do have their fair share of problems. Don't long for something you don't fully comprehend, he always told me," African Fig says.

"Thanks for sharing with me, and with Lion for that matter," Lucky says as he thanks African Fig.

"I know Lion often wishes he was a leopard. Leopard males have the thrill of hunting. In Lion's pride that thrill is mostly reserved for lionesses that do the hunting. Leopards don't have the stress associated with ruling the kingdom. Lion believes that leopards have it all, so your story is sure to bring Lion to new insights."

"I'm glad I could help, Lucky," African Fig says as he opens his leaves for the night. "Can you return a favor by getting the *Bushveld Times* delivered to these parts? I can't wait this long for the latest news anymore."

"I will ask Lion to pull some strings," Lucky says as he bids his friend farewell.

18

Owl's Curves of Emotions

Lucky notices a trail of fresh animal tracks in the game path he follows. The tracks closely resemble his own. "Must be some long lost and distant relative," Lucky thinks. So he continues to follow them.

He follows the tracks for about fifteen minutes until they come to an abrupt end close to a grove of marula trees. The trail stops so suddenly that it looks as if the animal had taken flight. Lucky circles the last pair of tracks in the hope of picking up the trail again.

"Looking for someone?" a voice asks from the direction of the marula trees.

Lucky looks up and spots an owl perched on one of the branches. "No one in particular," he responds. "I thought these tracks belonged to a distant relative of mine. My name is Lucky, by the way. Who are you?"

"I am Owl. I'm a professor in animal behavior at the University of the Bushveld."

"Should you not be sleeping with the sun being up?" Lucky asks curiously.

"I probably should be, but then I'll never observe the behavior of daytime animals. What brings you to these parts, Lucky?"

"I have been tasked by Lion to find out as much as possible about happiness. I need to report back to him with my findings before the rainy season starts."

"You're quite fortunate to cross my path then," Owl says. "Happiness is one of the subjects I teach to my animal psychology students. Do you have time for an abridged version of my class?"

"I absolutely do," Lucky says, getting comfortable against the trunk of a nearby marula tree. He almost cannot believe his luck.

"Happiness is best explained using a picture," Owl begins. "I refer to this picture as the 'Curve of Emotions.' It shows the spectrum of emotions someone can experience. It ranges from depression to ecstasy and spans any period in the animal's life.

"An extract from my life will illustrate just how much these curves can teach us about happiness.

"Driving to work is generally an unhappy activity for me. When I drove to work on Wednesday, for example, I experienced a sequence of events. You can follow these events on the curve as I explain them," Owl says. He unfolds a leaf with a graph on it.

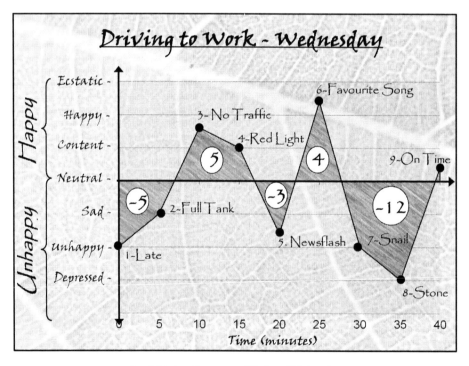

Leaf 18.1 – Driving to Work on Wednesday

"At the beginning of this sequence of events, I got into my car and realized I was *late*. This realization made me *unhappy*. Five minutes into my journey, however, I noticed my *tank* was *full*. This made me feel better. I was no longer *unhappy* but still a bit *sad*, realizing I would be late.

"After ten minutes, I reached the first major intersection on my route. There was no traffic. It was a school holiday. Most animals were on holiday, and the resultant lack of traffic and open roads lifted my spirits to somewhere between *happy* and *content*," Owl continued.

"After fifteen minutes, I approached a traffic light. It turned red just as I approached. I had to stop and lost valuable time. My level of happiness dropped to being *content*.

"Twenty minutes into my journey, a twelve percent increase in the fuel price was announced on the radio. The newsflash made me *unhappy*, but my favorite songs played shortly afterward, which made me *very happy*.

"My happiness was shortlived, however. I got stuck behind a snail inching along in the fast lane. I was frustrated and *unhappy*. While waiting to overtake the snail, it kicked up a stone that cracked my windshield. My mood plummeted and I was *depressed* momentarily. Money saved for a family holiday now had to go toward replacing the windshield.

"Finally, forty minutes after leaving home, I arrived at work. Having made it on time, despite all that happened, made me feel significantly better. I was feeling somewhere between *sad* and *content*.

"So that's the sequence of events, Lucky. The detail may have been a bit long-winded," Owl says. "It has, however, laid the foundation for some fascinating observations we can make from the curve.

"First, look at the gray surface areas enclosed between the curve and the time axis. You will see five such areas shaded in the graph," Owl says.

"I have indicated the relative size of each enclosed area on the graph, being -5, 5, -3, 4 and -12. Adding the sizes together gives an overall enclosed area of -11. The negative means the *overall* experience is an unhappy one. Therefore my *net* experience was 11 unhappy minutes while driving to work.

"Secondly," Owl continues, "although the net effect of driving to work is one of unhappiness, all isn't doom and gloom. There are moments of happiness along the way whenever the graph goes above the neutral horizontal axis. Around the time of realizing there was no traffic, I had five happy minutes. I had another four happy minutes around the time of hearing my favorite song.

"You can see that unhappy *events* can contain happy *moments*. By spotting these moments, rather than just seeing the overall unhappy event, we can be happier altogether.

"The opposite is also true," Owl says. "The Curve of Emotion for winning the lottery, for example, won't be one of bliss alone. The *overall* emotion may be one of happiness, but there will be unhappiness along the way. Misplacing the ticket, paying the taxes, and feeling the pressure to share winnings with family and friends will all detract from the overall happiness.

"Another interesting observation is the role our mood plays," Owl continues. "This Curve of Emotion on Leaf 18.2 shows the emotion I experienced when driving to work on May eleventh. This was a Friday, two days after the curve discussed earlier.

"The dotted line shows how my curve looked on Wednesday. The solid line shows the curve on Friday when my mood was much better. The solid and dotted lines represent the exact same events, just on different days with different moods.

"My emotions of Wednesday are superimposed on my Friday good mood. See how the unhappy areas are now smaller and the happy areas bigger than they were on Wednesday?" Owl says, full of excitement.

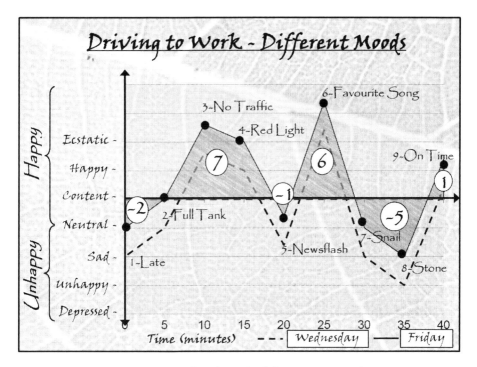

Leaf 18.2 – Effect of Mood While Driving to Work

"Adding these relative areas of -2, 7, -1, 6, -5 and 1 together gives a total of plus 6 happy minutes, making the overall event a happy one," Owl says.

"Once again the opposite is also true. A foul mood aggravates any unhappy encounters while lessening the impact of happy ones."

"Happiness is as old as Creation itself, yet we still struggle to define and understand it," Lucky says. Your graphs will go a long way in explaining happiness to Lion. They certainly have done so for me."

"I'm glad they helped, Lucky," Owl says. "You must excuse me, however, as it's way past my bedtime already. I have done enough animal observations for today."

Lucky bids farewell to Owl and heads off into the Bushveld to continue his adventure.

19

Tough Criticism to Swallow

Walking past the face of a cliff, Lucky sees a swallow busily adding another layer of mud and saliva to his nest underneath an overhanging rock.

"He must have seen so many things on his winter migrations. I'm sure he will have some new perspectives on happiness," Lucky thinks, so he stops and introduces himself.

"Well, it sure is a pleasure to meet you, sir," the bird says. "My name is Swallow. I'm an intelligence operative for the Circle of Bushveld Elders.

"There was a time when human beings did nothing for nature conservation. It was the time before fishing quotas and hunting regulations existed. Humans were steadily exterminating all animal species on earth.

"It was in those dark days that the Circle of Bushveld Elders tasked all swallows to gather intelligence on humans," Swallow explains.

"The objective was simple. We were to gather all intelligence we could lay our claws on. Every bit of information was considered valuable and sent to the Central Indexing Authority, or the CIA as we called it.

"The CIA selected and then categorized information that could be used for identifying human weaknesses. A separate division developed strategies to ensure the survival of all animal species against the onslaught of humans. These were the early days of operation Go Home, Sapiens. It became part of every swallow's life in the Bushveld.

"We had countless operatives all over the world. We studied human behavior and observed all forms of media in our quest to find their weaknesses."

"I can't believe this!" Lucky says in awe, with his lower jaw almost resting on his chest. "That's the stuff movies are made of. And all of it happened right here in our very own Bushveld, without us even knowing about it."

"You must have watched the Human Planet channel on television?" Swallow asks. "The purpose of this channel was to equip every animal with broad knowledge about humans. The aim was to empower animals so they could protect themselves against humans, should the need ever arise.

"Although we found no human weaknesses that would ensure our survival, we did make some interesting observations on various topics, including happiness. These observations are thought-provoking human mistakes we can learn from.

"This is our draft report," Swallow says as he opens a thick book. "I will page through and stop at sections relating to happiness."

Human Observation #23
Humans are the only creatures that show their teeth when they are happy.

Human Observation #48
Humans idolize their celebrities. They believe celebrities have perfect lives and that they are always happy. However, some of their celebrities were so unhappy they committed suicide, the ultimate act of unhappiness. Some of these celebrities were:

Cleopatra (30 BC)—Queen of Egypt,
Ernest Hemingway (1961)—American novelist,
Hannibal (182 BC)—Carthaginian military commander,
Jeff Alm (1993)—NFL player,
Kurt Cobain (1994)—lead singer of the band Nirvana,
Marc Anthony (30 BC)—Roman general and politician,
Michael (Awesome) Alfonso (2007)—professional wrestler,

Nafisa Joseph (2004)—Miss Universe 1997 semi-finalist,
Prince Alfred of Edinburgh (1899)—member of the British Royal Family,
Rudolph Diesel (1913)—inventor of the diesel engine, and
Socrates (399 BC)—Greek philosopher.

Human Observation #59a

Humans think money will make them happy. However, some humans' lives took a turn for the worse after winning lotteries. Some notable examples are:

Billie Bob Harrell Jr. committed suicide two years after winning $37 million in the Texas lottery in 1997. He realized he was unable to fix his marriage, which was under strain following his uncontrollable spending habits.

Jeffrey Dampier Jr. won $20 million in the Illinois lottery in 1996. He was then kidnapped and murdered, allegedly by his sister-in-law.

Gerald Muswagon won the $10 million lottery jackpot in 1998. He hanged himself in his parents' garage in 2005 after run-ins with the law and squandering most of his winnings.

Human Observation #59b

Coins like the ones humans use today only came into use in the seventh century BC. If money really makes humans happy, then it stands to reason that all people living prior to the seventh century BC were unhappy. This clearly could not be the case, so money cannot make people happy.

Human Observation #59c

Some humans gather money half their lives only to realize it does not make them happy. They then spend the remainder of their lives giving this hard-earned money away, hoping it will bring happiness once again. A strange phenomenon for a strange species!

Human Observation #68
Humans do not count their blessings often enough.

Nearly three billion people live on less than $2.50 a day, yet those earning more are not always happy.

Approximately twenty-five thousand people die every day from hunger or hunger-related causes, yet those with food are not always happy.

Close to a billion people entered the twenty-first century without being able to read a book, yet those who can read do not appreciate the fact enough.

It is estimated that around thirty-seven million people were blind in 2002, yet those who can see do not appreciate the fact enough.

Human Observation #77
Some experts believe it takes only seventeen muscles to smile and forty-three to frown. Others believe it takes twenty-six muscles to smile and sixty-two to frown. The actual number of muscles is irrelevant. There appears to be consensus that less effort is required to show happiness than is required to show unhappiness.

Human Observation #84
Results from the World Values Survey show the top five happiest countries in the world are Nigeria, Mexico, Venezuela, El Salvador, and Puerto Rico.

Humans from these countries are generally not very wealthy.

Human Observation #92
The personal income of Americans has increased more than two and a half times over the last fifty years, but their happiness level has remained the same.

Human Observation #98
Thirty-seven percent of the people on Forbes's list of wealthiest Americans are less happy than the average American.

Human Observation #112
Colors affect the mood of humans. Bright colors such as yellow reflect more light and may cause irritability. Green is the most soothing color. Human studies have shown that people working in a green environment experience fewer headaches and other signs of sickness and fatigue.

Human Observation #115
Vitamin D deficiency may result in, or lead to, depression. The human body creates vitamin D when exposed to direct sunlight. This may explain why some people feel more miserable during winter when their exposure to sunlight is less.

Human Observation #142
The human body releases endorphins when exercising. Endorphins are natural stimulants that give humans a high.

"This makes for really good reading," Lucky says while scribbling in his notebook. "And here we were sometimes envying humans as the crown of creation. They really have some issues to work through."

"They do, sir," Swallow replies. "You must please excuse me now, as I must complete my nest before the rainy season starts."

"I have the same deadline, Swallow, so I'll leave you to it," Lucky says as he heads off again in search of happiness.

20

Driving Buffalo's Happiness

L ucky gazes across the Bushveld from his vantage point on a hill. When he finally spots a water hole, he wastes no time and leaves the mountainous terrain for the plains below.

After a strenuous walk, Lucky reaches the outskirts of the water hole. He climbs a red ivory tree from where he surveys his surroundings for predators.

"Nothing except for a lone buffalo," Lucky concludes and heads down the tree to the water hole. Buffaloes are no threat to rats. Lone buffaloes like this one, however, are generally temperamental. When the herd kicks them out, they love to sulk and look for ways to vent their frustration.

Lucky plays it safe and heads to the edge of the water hole opposite the buffalo. "Mind if I share?" Lucky asks as the buffalo stares straight at him.

"Go ahead, but I don't want any noise," the buffalo says.

"Looks like you had a rough day," Lucky says while evaluating possible escape routes.

"I've had a rough year," the buffalo replies abruptly.

A deadly silence envelops the water hole. The quiet uneasiness that develops drags on and on until it eventually becomes unbearable.

"And how was the year before that?" Lucky eventually erupts with the first halfway decent thing that pops into his head.

"It was also rough! In fact, every year is rough. You see, I'm a market analyst. Well, I used to be one. My employer retrenched me following the economic crisis of 2008. I'm only thirty-two years old and have not accumulated enough retirement pension yet. I'm currently doing ad hoc consulting work, but I struggle to pay the bills. What's your story?" the buffalo says.

"My name is Lucky and I'm a math teacher. I have been sent by Lion himself to find out as much as possible about happiness," he says. "You sure look like you could do with some of the advice I have heard from other animals."

"I am Buffalo. Thanks for the offer, but maybe some other time. I'm not one to take advice. I give advice. Do you want my advice, Lucky?" Buffalo asks.

"I definitely do," Lucky replies with the only possible answer to Buffalo's question.

"I was recently contracted by swallows to analyze data they collected on humans. They wanted to develop a strategy to counter the human onslaught on nature," Buffalo says.

"My work focused on human spending habits and market trends. One particularly interesting trend emerged from the data I analyzed. The graph shows what humans believe it costs to make them happy.

"Now the pages I'm about to show you are highly classified. They're intended for Lion's eyes only once the Bushveld Elders approve the content. Since you also work for Lion, I'm happy to share the information with you," Buffalo says and walks around the water hole to meet up with Lucky.

On a smooth patch of mud next to Lucky, Buffalo draws a table with his front hoof. "This table shows the iconic means of transport for different human age groups," he begins. "Each age group believes that having the corresponding transport mode will make it happy.

"The table essentially shows the money required to make each age group happy when using transport modes as the yardstick. Don't worry too much about the purchase prices shown for each item. These prices are sure to have escalated since I did the analyses."

Age Group	Mode of Transport	Purchase Price
Teens	Bicycle	$200
Twenties	Motorcycle	$4 000
Thirties	Family Sedan	$20 000
Forties	Sports Utility Vehicle	$65 000
Fifties	Convertible	$220 000
Sixties	Motor Yacht	$550 000

Mud Patch 20.1 – Monetary Cost of Happiness by Age Group

Buffalo continues, "Nice table you might think. But only once it's plotted on the graph you see in this mud patch, does it unveil the predicament faced by humans.

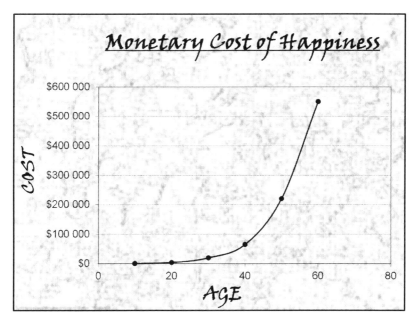

Mud Patch 20.2 – Monetary Cost of Happiness Graph

"Although this graph is based on human behavior, all animals can benefit from what it tells us.

"This graph proves that money can never make us happy, Lucky," Buffalo says as he starts showing emotion for the first time. "We've suspected it all along, but now we have mathematical proof."

"It's beautiful," Lucky sighs in appreciation of the fine work Buffalo has done. "As we grow older, we need more and more money to make us happy," he adds, pointing to the curve.

"Indeed," Buffalo concurs. "You have probably also noticed it's an exponential curve; the gradient becomes steeper as we grow older. This of course means that at a young age, only a bit more money is required to make us happy.

"As we grow older, however, the incremental amounts of money needed to maintain happiness spirals out of control. Eventually in the latter years of life, it takes massive amounts of money to make us happy.

"All of this holds true, only if we choose money as the source of our happiness," Buffalo says. "If we let other things make us happy, then the curve doesn't apply to us and we're free from the gloomy future it paints."

"Your work is outstanding, Buffalo," Lucky commends him. "If this was the only thing you ever achieved in life, you would have done well. The Animal Kingdom will forever be indebted to you. Your work has saved a million others from chasing money in vain for their happiness."

"Your words are kind, my friend" Buffalo says with a tone completely opposite of when they first met. "If you ever visit these parts again, I will invite you for a drink at this water hole. You have made me feel useful again after all these years of solitude."

"I will take you up on that drink, Buffalo," Lucky says. "And if you ever visit the African Bushveld Technical Academy, you need to give this same lecture to my students. I will be privileged to have you as a guest lecturer."

With these words, Lucky and Buffalo go their separate ways, both reflecting on the unique encounter they just experienced.

21

A Vulture with Attitude

Lucky has walked for two days to cross the Sua salt pan, but the edge of the pan still eludes him. He feels the sun draining the very last reserves from his body. Images of his wife and children flash before his eyes. These images keep him sane; these images keep him moving.

The relentless pull of gravity eventually gets the upper hand and Lucky collapses while sending a cloud of dust into the air as he hits the ground.

It could have been minutes. It could have been hours. Barely conscious, Lucky cracks open one eye as the soothing cool relief of a shadow touches his face.

His eyes struggle to focus amid the searing light. In front of him lurks the owner of the shadow. A giant hooded vulture. Lucky jumps up at the sight with energy reserves squeezed from somewhere deep inside.

"Is this how it's going to end?" Lucky thinks. He closes his eyes, hoping that reality will disappear.

"Don't worry, son. Today is your lucky day," the vulture says in response to Lucky's visible anguish. "I saw an ad the other day promoting the benefits of fresh produce. Apparently it's a lot healthier than red meat. Less cholesterol or something."

"Good old marketers," Lucky says, smiling.

"Anyway, the name is Vulture. I'm a greengrocer by trade and a vegetarian by choice. I'm here to help as it sure looks like you need a little helping."

Vulture gently takes hold of Lucky in his claws. With one flap of his giant wings, the two of them become airborne and rise high above the vast expanse of Sua Pan.

"I'm flying!" Lucky thinks. He smiles, remembering Elephant's story on how a crisis presents danger and opportunity. "From almost dead to flying for the first time ever. This has got to be one of the craziest days of my life."

Vulture swoops down and lands on the banks of the Boteti River where Lucky wastes no time in quenching his thirst. Once he has had enough, he takes another mouthful, just in case.

"I'm forever in your debt, Vulture. My name is Lucky," he says, holding out his front right paw.

"The pleasure is all mine, Lucky. But tell me, son, how does a seemingly sane, wingless animal get the idea in his head to cross Sua Pan on foot?"

"I'm on a quest for Lion to find out whatever I can about happiness. I thought there would be different perspectives from animals this side of the pan. What's the key to happiness to you, Vulture?"

"Attitude, son. It's all about attitude," Vulture responds without hesitation. "I have seen it. Different animals can go through the exact same experience, but their attitude ultimately makes the experience good or bad. Your attitude determines whether you're happy or not.

"I tell you what, while you try emptying the river, I will tell you a story. You can then be the judge on attitude and happiness."

"Sounds good to me," Lucky responds and then sits back to listen.

"When my two sons were still young, we brought their food to the nest. We cared for and protected them until the day arrived when we had to kick them out of the nest.

"I should add at this point that our nest is on the fourteenth ledge of the Sheer Cliff Apartments complex. We have the best views from our nest because it's located on one of the highest ledges in the Bushveld.

"Anyway," Vulture continues, "we wanted to give our children an equal start in life, so on the count of three, my wife kicked the one and I the other out of the nest. Some think that is cruel, but it's the vulture way. Until research on parenting proves otherwise, I believe this approach to be the only way for young chicks to take up the responsibility of caring for themselves.

"As they fell down, our eldest chick screamed at us and gave us a stare I remember to this day. He flapped his wings profusely and crash-landed eight ledges down from our nest. He just sat there, either sulking or cursing at us. It was tough seeing your child so helpless, but that's Nature's way.

"He sat on that sixth ledge for two solid days. Hunger must have eventually forced him to take the final plunge, which again was accompanied with a lot of cursing.

"He crash-landed near the foot of the cliff but was unscathed. He then hopped to the foot of the cliff where the sulking continued in the shade of an overhanging ledge.

"Our youngest chick, on the other hand," Vulture continues, "cried with a joy that echoed his freedom as he left the nest. Rather than looking back at us, his eyes surveyed the new and exciting world around him.

"Just like our eldest, he crash-landed on the sixth ledge where he rested his wings for a while. Shortly thereafter, he took another plunge in what seemed to us like a jump of joy.

"His landing was hard, but once he had his wits about him, he immediately tried flying again. I will always remember how he hopped and clapped, hopped and clapped until eventually he disappeared from view into a thicket of bush willow trees.

"We saw our youngest again thirty minutes later when he soared past our nest. He had the look on his face of someone who had conquered the world.

"We never saw our eldest again. Some say that Jackal took him, but we choose to believe he is flying up there with the eagles.

"Anyway, Lucky," Vulture says as he clears a lump from his throat, "our sons had the same experience, from being kicked out of the nest to crashing at the foot of the cliff. There was, however, a big difference in their attitude.

"Our eldest was negative from the start and didn't enjoy the experience as a result. Our youngest was bold. Despite facing the same adversity as his brother, he chose to be positive. Not only did he succeed in flying, but he also gained happiness from his experience. He didn't allow his fear to rob him of his joy."

"Was it not perhaps a fear of heights that set them apart, Vulture?" Lucky asks.

"No, son. We are vultures. We don't carry that gene. Their attitude set them apart. A good, positive attitude goes a long way in determining whether we enjoy what we do."

"I think I can relate to your hypothesis," Lucky says. "When I'm in a good mood, I hardly notice driving in rush-hour traffic. When I'm agitated, however, the mere sight of rush-hour traffic brings my blood to a boil."

"There you have it," Vulture says. "Let me go one step further to illustrate my point. What comes to mind when you see the word 'HAPPINESSISNOWHERE'?" Vulture scratches the word on the soft bark of a nearby fever tree.

"I see … that happiness is *nowhere*. My quest is in vain as I won't find happiness anywhere?" Lucky hesitantly attempts the obvious.

"Could be," Vulture says with a know-it-all tone in his voice. "It could also spell 'happiness is *now here*' if you insert the spaces differently. How you look at things determines what you will see, Lucky. A positive outlook gives a different result."

"That's a good one, Vulture." Lucky chuckles. "It will definitely be one of the pranks I pull on Lion when giving him feedback."

"Prank?" Vulture asks. "Think of it more as a social experiment."

"I will do that, Vulture. Thanks for your advice, and thanks for saving my life. I'm forever in your debt," Lucky says, trying to pick up his water-filled stomach. "And if I ever do come across a cursing vulture, I will send him your way."

22

The Predicament of Jackal's Life

The ground trembles as a bolt of lightning briefly connects heaven and earth. "I need to find shelter or get fried tonight," Lucky thinks.

He looks around frantically and spots the entrance to a cave not far away. He rushes toward the cave as fast as his legs can carry him.

At the cave's entrance, Lucky pauses for a moment. It smells a bit moldy but still beats facing the raging storm outside. Lucky walks deeper into the cave to get out of the chilly draft.

He enters an enormous passage heading into the heart of the Waterberg Mountains. At the first bend in the passage, the flickering shadow of an animal against the passage wall greets Lucky.

"Mind if I share the cave with you until the storm passes?" Lucky asks. He still hasn't seen the other animal, but the sound of his own voice calms him amid the uneasy silence.

"I don't mind at all, stranger. Come and warm yourself here by the fire," echoes a friendly, reassuring voice from within the mountain.

By now, Lucky has walked far enough to see the silhouette of the voice etched against the backlight of a warm and inviting fire.

"My name is Lucky."

"I am Jackal" comes the reply. "And what brings you to this part of the Bushveld?"

"I'm in search of happiness. Actually, any advice from any animal on happiness is what I'm after. I need to report back to Lion before the rainy season starts, and by the looks of this thunderstorm, I don't have much time left."

"I might be able to help you," Jackal replies. "I have lived a long and good life, most of it as a stockbroker. I retired three rainy seasons ago, and now I'm writing my memoirs. I want to leave something for my grandchildren to guide them through life.

"My memoirs have a section that ties up nicely with your search for happiness," Jackal continues. "I call the section 'The Predicament of Life.' It's actually my favorite chapter. It illustrates, with one simple graph, the constant battle we wage between *wanting* and *having*.

"Walk with me," Jackal says as he lights a bundle of bushman's candles to light the wall of the cave.

"*This*, my friend, is the predicament of life," Jackal says, pointing to a graph on the wall.

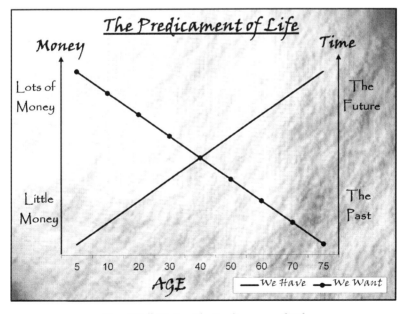

Cave Wall 22.1 – The Predicament of Life

"This graph compares our *wants* to our *haves* as we continue through life," Jackal says.

"But rather than boring you with theory, I will explain the graph at hand. Although my life was the basis for developing this graph, the principles it portrays apply to animals and humans alike.

"Let's rewind to when I was fifteen years old. You can follow my story if you look at this version of the graph," Jackal says as he casts the light onto an adjacent graph.

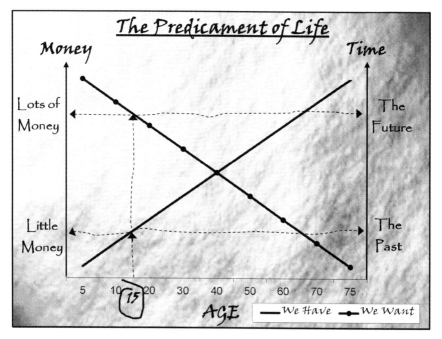

Cave Wall 22.2 – The Predicament of Life at 15

"At the age of fifteen, I had hopes and dreams like every young child. I *wanted* two things: lots of money and the future. The future I wanted was me all grown up with my driver's license and being my own boss. I also *wanted* lots of money to get a sports car and other expensive things to impress my friends. Mostly, I wanted to impress the vixens.

"What I *had* at fifteen was exactly the opposite," Jackal says. "I *had* very little money, but I also *had* the past. Though not fully appreciated at the time, having the past meant I *had* health, vitality, and simplicity in my life. I *had* food and a place to sleep, courtesy of my parents. I didn't have worries or bills to pay. My whole life lay ahead of me.

"But life continued, and before I knew it, I turned forty. If you look at this version of the graph, you will see becoming forty is quite a unique event," Jackal says as he moves deeper into the cave.

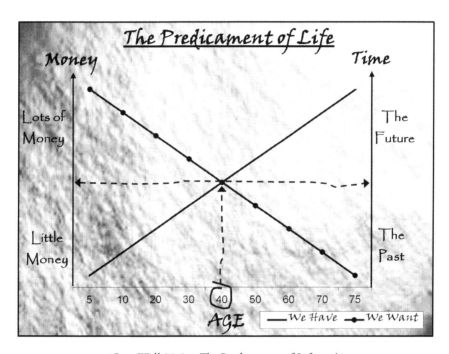

Cave Wall 22.3 – The Predicament of Life at 40

"At the age of forty, the two curves on the graph intersect each other. At this intersection, my *wants* equaled my *haves*. I finally had what I wanted and wanted what I had.

At forty, I didn't *want* little or lots of money. I was somewhere in the middle. I realized there was more to life than having lots of money. I knew, however, that if I had too little money, I would see my children go hungry and risk having insufficient retirement pension.

"When I was forty, I no longer wanted the future as badly as when I was fifteen. I realized life was too precious and short to wish it away. After all, I already had reached the halfway mark of mine.

"Now here is the best part of this whole graph, Lucky," Jackal says. He lights two more bushman's candles as if to stress the importance of what is to come.

"As far as I know, this is the first graph that proves why we experience a midlife crisis."

The empty stare from Lucky that meets Jackal's excitement prompts his reply: "I probably need to explain."

"During the first half of life, the gap between the two curves steadily diminished as I approached forty. You can see it here," Jackal says as he lights up the graph.

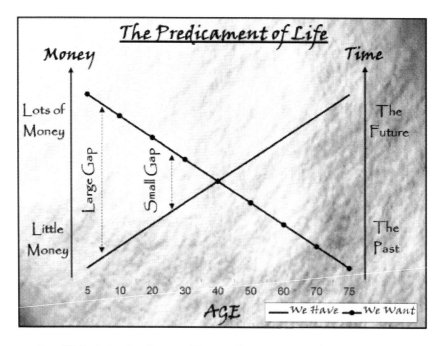

Cave Wall 22.4 – Gap Between Wants and Haves Diminishes Approaching 40

"Eventually the curves intersected when I reached forty. After forty years and hard work, I eliminated the gap. I finally had what I wanted and wanted what

I had, albeit in moderation.

"So what was next for me? What do you do with the second half of life when you already have what you want, and want what you have?

"This uncertainty spelled a midlife crisis for me. I didn't set goals for myself past the age of forty. There was little more to achieve, so there was only a little more to want. Up until now, the things I wanted gave me purpose. My purpose was to satisfy those wants. My life lost that purpose when I turned forty, and thus I was having a midlife crisis.

"That's half the truth," Jackal says with a smile that could light up the cave by itself. "This curve also proves that life begins at forty! It may sound like a contradiction to the midlife crisis explanation of earlier, but hear me out.

"Looking at the graph again, I had two things in moderation at forty. I had a fair amount of money, and I also had half of my life ahead of me.

"What could be better than this?" Jackal asks. "I worked to get what I wanted for forty years and finally got it, albeit only in moderation.

"Now, I finally had enough money to buy some of the things I always wanted. I was also still young and healthy enough to enjoy life and the things I had. My life only really began at forty!"

"It's uncanny how accurately this graph represents life," Lucky says.

"It is, isn't it," Jackal says. "But it doesn't stop there."

"After the age of forty, the two curves start diverging. What I *had* and what I *wanted* started growing apart.

"This version of the graph shows my life when I was sixty-five years old," Jackal says, pointing to the graph.

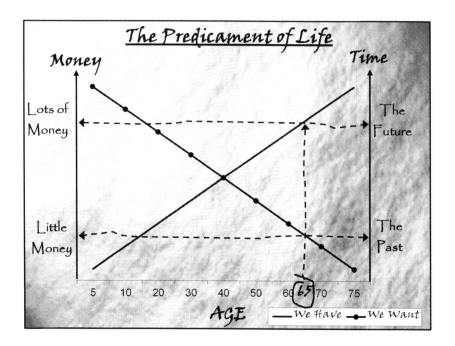

Cave Wall 22.5 – Predicament of Life at 65

"At sixty-five I finally had lots of money. I also had the future I so badly wanted as a fifteen-year-old. My problem was that my wants had also changed. At sixty-five I wanted the past and what it represented: the health, youth, vitality, and carefreeness of a fifteen-year-old.

"Money didn't bother me anymore. I only wanted a little bit of money to get by, as I didn't need much more. I already accumulated the possessions I wanted, and I was getting too old anyway to go on elaborate and expensive holidays.

"I had come to the realization that there was more to life than money. I no longer wanted money as badly as when I was fifteen."

"I understand now why you call it the predicament of life," Lucky says. "Apart from when we're forty, we never seem to have what we want, nor want what we have! It's a constant battle."

"You're right, but that's not necessarily a bad thing," Jackal says. "If we have what we want for too long, we eventually stagnate and become complacent. Wanting more stimulates hard work, innovation, and progression. Wanting more is inherently part of what we are.

"My advice is to accept the fact that we'll want things throughout our lives. What we have now may not be exactly what we want, but we should enjoy and appreciate what it gives us regardless. It won't be there forever."

"Your memoirs truly give back something to the Animal Kingdom, Jackal," Lucky says. "It sounds like the storm has passed. I need to hit the road again to be back in time to report to Lion. Thanks for sharing your memories with me.

"By the way, is there anything in your memoirs about vultures?" Lucky asks.

"Nothing, but why do you ask?" Jackal responds.

"I met Vulture a few days ago. His eldest is missing, and he still has hopes of finding him one day. He said rumors are circulating that you took him. It would be great to give him some closure if that isn't the case."

"As scavengers, vultures and jackals have a mutual respect for each other. We'll only eat each other, I suppose, as a last and desperate resort. I have only ever seen vultures from a distance, so you can give your friend that reassurance."

"I will do that, Jackal," Lucky says as he leaves the cave to continue his journey home.

23

Ostrich's Essential Unhappiness

"Home! Almost there," Lucky thinks as he recognizes the bluish-gray silhouette of Iron Mountain in the distance. "I wonder how …"

A sniveling sound interrupts Lucky's thoughts. He stops and then continues to walk around a patch of tamboti trees toward the sobbing. Here Lucky spots an ostrich staring at the remnants of her nest. Eggshells litter the area surrounding it.

"Are you all right there, ma'am?" Lucky asks.

"I'm fine, but my eggs are not," Ostrich says with tears rolling down her beak. Her long neck curves downward from her body, with her head positioned slightly off the ground and above the eggshells.

"Maybe I can help you," Lucky says. "My name is Lucky. For quite a few full moons now, I have traveled the Bushveld searching for happiness. I have learned a great deal, and I'm sure I have something that will cheer you up."

"And what makes you think I need cheering up?" Ostrich asks.

"Well, don't you want to be happy rather than miserable?" Lucky asks.

"I do, but being unhappy is just as important," Ostrich replies.

Lucky pauses at this illogical response and then repeats his question from earlier to make sure he heard right. "Are you all right there, ma'am?"

"I'm still fine, Lucky. However, you seem skeptical about the importance of *un*happiness in life. Maybe you still have something more to learn about happiness. Let me paint you a picture to illustrate the importance of *un*happiness."

"I remain to be convinced, but you have my undivided attention," Lucky says.

"Suppose every place on earth has the same temperature," Ostrich starts. "In this world, the words *hot* and *cold* have no meaning, because, after all, everything has the same temperature.

"Suppose then the temperature in the Arctic decreases while remaining the same everywhere else. Now, and only now, can we refer to the Arctic region as being cold. Why is this? Because now, and only now, is the rest of the globe *relatively* warmer than the Arctic region.

"The temperature imbalance was first required to give meaning to the words *hot* and *cold*. Cold, being the one extreme, only found meaning once the other extreme of warmth found its meaning. The one extreme can't exist without the other.

"Happiness is certainly no different. Happiness after all is an extreme emotion, with unhappiness being the other extreme. Happiness only exists because unhappiness exists. It's therefore essential to be unhappy at times so we can be happy during other times."

"You make a very convincing argument, Ostrich. I can see this principle in my own life," Lucky says. "I miss my children while at work, a form of unhappiness. I'm then happy to see them when I return in the evening.

"Following your reasoning then, Ostrich, I'm happy to see them because I was unhappy while I was away from them. Being unhappy was initially required in order to be happy later on."

"There you go! You caught on quickly," Ostrich says with a grin.

"I think it's rather a case of you being a good teacher," Lucky says as he scribbles a few notes in his book.

"Thanks for sharing your wisdom, Ostrich. I wish you better luck with your new nest. If you ever need protection for it, I can introduce you to Dung Beetle. He is the reigning Bushveld bodybuilding champion. Nobody will bother you or your eggs when he is around. That I can assure you," Lucky says as he sets off in the direction of Iron Mountain.

24

Reporting Back to Lion

Lucky reaches the passage through Iron Mountain as the wind gathers clouds into a big gray mass that fills the heavens. The summer rains have arrived.

"This is the end of my adventure. I have made it back in time," Lucky thinks.

He continues through the passage to the valley beyond, which is home.

The encounters and discussions he has had replay in his mind as he heads in the direction of Lion's den. "I hope I don't disappoint him. I hope what I have learned will help him," Lucky thinks as he reaches the outskirts of the den.

Lucky spots Lion staring across the savannah. The picture is almost a carbon copy of how he left Lion when his journey began. Lucky walks toward him and takes a seat on a rock next to Lion.

"I see you made full use of the time available, Lucky," Lion says while glancing at the heavens. "It's good to have you back in one piece."

"It's good to be back home, Lion. I have learned and seen so much."

"I'm all ears, Lucky," Lion says. "My situation hasn't improved since you left, and I sincerely hope your mission wasn't in vain."

"Before I start, Lion, I should mention that Impala humbly requested a grace period for him and his herd—in return for his valuable advice on happiness, of course," Lucky says.

"Let's not discuss such important matters on an empty stomach, Lucky. I will give it some consideration after you brief me and after I have eaten," Lion says. "What should I do to be happy?"

"Happiness is a very complex emotion," Lucky begins. "It's impossible to give you a one-liner, or even a short summary, on how to be happy, Lion. I have learned that happiness means different things to different animals. Different things also make different animals happy.

"I have summarized what I have learned in my report entitled 'Lucky Go Happy,'" he says, handing the report to Lion.

"You will see from the report that each animal has a piece of the happiness puzzle. There is a lesson to be learned from each and every one of my encounters with them.

"I learned that the unhappiness you're experiencing is an essential part of life. A permanent state of happiness also doesn't exist, so it's pointless yearning for it.

"Many of the animals did however give me valuable advice on introducing more happiness into *your* life. It's all there in my report."

"I will read your report then, Lucky," Lion says as he turns the cover page. "Go and spend time with your family. I will let you know my thoughts on your report and Impala's request as soon as I'm ready."

During the next few days, Lion came to understand the concept of happiness much better. Although he remained a sucker for advertising campaigns and did not give up his anti-dandruff shampoo, he applied many of the lessons from Lucky's report to his own life. Lion made happiness happen for himself and his subjects, and affectionately became known as the Contented King.